TABLE OF CONTENTS

U.S. GLOBAL ENGAGEMENT & RELIGION

The first page of the most recent National Security Strategy (NSS) advises that "to succeed, we must face the world as it is."[1] Increasingly, the foreign policy community has recognized that the world is often—and powerfully—shaped by religion.[2]

Many U.S government initiatives have acknowledged that effective global engagement requires improved understanding of religious dynamics. A 600-page Religious Engagement Report of the Interagency Working Group on Religion and Global Affairs has inventoried embassy engagement of religious communities abroad, and the White House's Office of Faith-based and Neighborhood Partnerships has committed to fostering interfaith cooperation and understanding.[3] The Joint Chiefs of Staff have appointed military chaplains to serve as advisors on religious affairs overseas,[4] and the U.S. Agency for International Development has developed a guide to help staff better understand conflict situations where religion is a factor.[5]

These initiatives reflect significant progress in the continuing U.S. effort to understand and engage religious factors. As experts have argued, the success of U.S. diplomacy in the next decade will be measured by "its ability to connect with the hundreds of millions of people throughout the world whose identity is defined by religion."[6]

Americans are well-positioned to connect with a religious world. Nearly 60 percent of Americans report that religion is "very important" in their lives, and about 40 percent attend a religious service at least once a week.[7] The United States is also the most religiously diverse country in the world. Beyond various Christian traditions, at least 14 major religious traditions are represented in America, in addition to the 16 percent of citizens who do not belong to any particular religion.[8] Half of Americans identify with one of dozens of Protestant denominations, but this proportion has declined as other religions are increasingly represented.[9]

America's Greatest Soft Power

America's religious diversity today is a result of its founders' conviction that individuals and communities should be allowed to hold and express their beliefs, publicly and without fear. This belief is the lens through which the U.S. government continues to view religion, both at home and abroad.

From the Rhode Island Charter and Virginia Statute of Religion to the First Amendment to the U.S. Constitution, the principle of religious liberty is central to the American story.[10] As President Barack Obama explained in Cairo in 2009, "Freedom in America is indivisible from the freedom to practice one's religion."[11] On Ramadan the following year, Obama called the United States "a nation where the ability of peoples of different faiths to coexist peacefully and with mutual respect for one another stands in contrast to the religious conflict that persists around the globe."[12]

A foundational domestic value, religious freedom has also become a foreign policy imperative. In his 1941 State of the Union Address, President Franklin D. Roosevelt declared that the United States sought to secure the "freedom of every person to worship God in his own way—everywhere in the world."[13] In 1948 Eleanor Roosevelt helped draft the Universal Declaration of Human Rights (UDHR), including an article affirming the right to freedom of thought, conscience and religion.[14] Half a century later, President Bill Clinton signed the International Religious Freedom Act (IRFA), codifying in U.S. law the promotion of this right overseas and condemnation of any violations of it.[15] Today, President Obama asserts that freedom of religion is "central to the ability of peoples to live together."[16]

That claim is more than mere rhetoric. Religious liberty has been statistically linked with economic development and democratic stability and its absence correlated with violent extremism and religious conflict and persecution.[17] For more than 60 years the international community has officially recognized religious freedom as a basic human right. That diplomatic commitment reflects a worldwide aspiration: The vast majority of global poll respondents say it is important that they live in a country where they can freely practice their religion.[18]

Given both its significance at home and endorsement abroad, freedom of religion has been called America's single greatest soft power.[19]

Soft power strategies, which spur change through attraction rather than coercion, will be one of many tools for promoting religious freedom; monitoring and condemning persecution and seeking the release of religious prisoners also play key roles.[20] But as President Obama noted in his Nobel Peace Prize speech: "The promotion of human rights cannot be about exhortation alone."[21] The first U.S. Ambassador-at-Large for International Religious Freedom, Robert Seiple, writes that "promotion of religious freedom has generated greater success…when this methodology is linked with vested self-interest."[22] And the first director of the State Department's International Religious Freedom Office, Thomas Farr, adds that in the long term, reactive approaches must be accompanied by "the systematic advancement of the idea that religious freedom can benefit every society and every people."[23] A soft-power approach acknowledges that high stakes—individual lives, societal development and international security—demand sophisticated engagement.[24]

This strategy must also emphasize the prevention of violations of religious freedom. Success requires unprecedented cooperation between advocates of religious freedom and of religious pluralism. Religious freedom is fundamentally linked to legal rights and cannot result solely from efforts to develop understanding.[25] At the same time, intolerance undermines religious freedom, and so conflict resolution and inter-religious understanding are necessary for true religious liberty.

To promote religious freedom as a soft power also means engaging communities in dialogue on difficult definitions of religion and disagreements over legal boundaries. An effective approach will account for a variety of theologies, principles and worldviews.

Global engagement is multidirectional, and U.S. government officials are placing increasing emphasis on listening to the audiences they intend to reach, identifying mutual interests and values, and adapting their approaches as necessary. Leadership does not mean imposing a particular political or social model, and influence begins with a deep understanding of the people America hopes to affect.[26]

Public Diplomacy and Religion

The tools of public diplomacy are ideally suited for a soft-power approach to religious freedom promotion that conveys American values, encourages mutual exchange and supports local social and cultural institutions that enable religious freedom.[27] Past efforts have recognized the importance of religion but have at times fallen short in engaging it. After September 11, 2001, public diplomacy played a resurgent role in U.S. foreign policy, particularly in Muslim-majority countries. But efforts to persuade those populations of shared values—often driven by concerns about Islam as a problem— instead alienated many Muslim audiences.

The new principles of global engagement call instead for a sharper focus on religious freedom, employing the best methods of public diplomacy.[28] The integration of public diplomacy and religious freedom promotion is critical to renewed efforts to rebuild lost trust as part of the post-Cairo-speech "New Beginning" initiative. And religious freedom is central to many of the 21st century's most important strategic issues, including post-conflict reconstruction, immigration and integration, women's rights, violent extremism, political Islam, and engagement of multilateral institutions and international law.

Successful public diplomacy—whether in articulating U.S. values, advocating for U.S. foreign policy, or shaping environments abroad to further U.S. interests—is inseparable from the issue of religious freedom. Public diplomacy must be informed by an understanding of religion and religious freedom, and religious freedom is significantly advanced through public diplomacy techniques.

In early 2010, Under Secretary of State for Public Diplomacy and Public Affairs Judith McHale released the "Global Strategic Plan for a New Public Diplomacy," outlining five strategic imperatives for public diplomacy in the 21st century.[29] They are:
- Shape the narrative
- Expand and strengthen people-to-people relationships
- Combat violent extremism
- Better inform policymaking
- Deploy resources in line with current priorities

Engagement with religious freedom can contribute particularly to the first three objectives.

Shape the Narrative
The first strategic imperative of public diplomacy is to "develop proactive outreach strategies to inform, inspire, and persuade."[30] While this requires significant media

engagement and rapid-response capabilities, it depends equally on the development of compelling content.[31] The primary driver of negative global opinion of the United States is disbelief in its government's commitment to democracy and human rights.[32] Only six percent of respondents in a poll of Arab countries, for example, said that the most important motivation for U.S. policy in the Middle East was spreading human rights. One-third thought its main objective was "weakening the Muslim world."[33]

Expand and Strengthen People-to-People Relationships
The second imperative calls on U.S. government officials to "build mutual trust and respect through expanded public diplomacy programs and platforms."[34] Past public diplomacy efforts have been criticized for emphasizing pop culture over substance. Moving forward, programs that engage religious topics are more likely to build effective relationships in a highly religious world. For decades, NGO-based experts have recognized the importance of religion-related discussion and exchange in building mutual understanding. Several have developed projects with international impact.[35]

Combat Violent Extremism
The third strategic imperative is to "counter violent extremist voices, discredit and delegitimize al Qaeda, and empower local credible voices."[36] Freedom of religion is a critical defense against extremism. Restrictions on freedom of expression and of religious practice tend to correlate with violence and instability, often in countries of strategic importance to the United States. In societies that support religious liberty, however, community leaders can undermine extremists' messages, pursue theological arguments for pluralism, and empower religious figures to guide efforts on development, health and education.[37]

Given the importance of religious freedom to those strategic imperatives, any U.S. official who engages in public diplomacy should be able to:
- Communicate the role of religion in American public life;
- Dispel misperceptions about the U.S. policy of promoting religious freedom; and
- Describe the benefits of increased religious freedom overseas.

This Resource Guide

This report highlights many successful efforts at the intersection of public diplomacy and religious freedom. A group of young Imams in Cairo extolled their U.S. Embassy-financed English-language training, explaining that they can now more fully participate in international discussions on the role of religion in public life. Two students from the Middle East on a State Department-sponsored visit to Philadelphia were convinced by their peers to attend a Jewish worship service. Diverse religious leaders from South and Southeast Asia have met, with U.S. government support, to share ideas for advancing human rights and development.

But despite stronger linkages between religious freedom and public diplomacy, government officials face constraints in fully implementing a public diplomacy-based approach to religious freedom promotion. Increasing recognition of the role of religion in international affairs has not alleviated remaining concerns about engagement with religious freedom. In some embassies, a bureaucratic gap separates Public Affairs Officers from diplomats tasked with religious freedom and human rights, and religious freedom can be a relatively inaccessible issue for public diplomacy officials.[38] Without clear guidance or dedicated funds, those without a personal interest in religious freedom may be unlikely to engage, and those who are motivated may have to acquire their own materials on an ad-hoc basis.[39]

To help fill that void, this resource will offer guidelines in identifying public diplomacy programs and activities to promote religious freedom. The guide is for any official engaging in public diplomacy, including but not limited to Public Affairs Officers and Cultural Affairs Officers.[40]

The ideas in this guide are based on a desk review, as well as extensive interviews in Bangladesh, Egypt, Greece, Qatar and the United States. More than 130 interviews were conducted with government officials, academics, human-rights activists, and civil-society and religious leaders. The interviews sought to assess:
- Current levels of training and programming related to religious freedom.
- Challenges that Foreign Service Officers face in promoting religious freedom.
- Resources that would be useful for government officials in this work.
- Best practices for promoting religious freedom and an increased understanding of both religious freedom in the United States and U.S. international religious freedom policy.
- Opportunities for collaboration among embassies and NGOs.

Drawing on interviewees' experience and insight, this guide outlines three broad steps for program-based promotion of religious freedom:[41]

1. Define Goals
The first section examines U.S. government activity around religious freedom and suggests potential roles for public diplomacy, including to:
- Reach citizens directly when bilateral efforts are not viable;
- Increase awareness of government restrictions, encouraging citizens to seek legal and political protections;
- Equip civil society to combat social hostilities;
- Promote a culture of religious freedom among younger generations; and
- Publicize positive local developments for religious freedom.

2. Shape Messaging
The second section summarizes recent research and data in outlining four major reasons for promoting religious freedom abroad, because it:
- Upholds an internationally recognized human right;
- Furthers national stability and international security;
- Contributes to economic development; and
- Promotes democratization.

It also captures practical and theoretical arguments addressing four common concerns about U.S. international religious freedom policy, that it:

- Defies separation of church and state;
- Constitutes a form of cultural imperialism;
- Protects only Christians; and
- Overstates U.S. legitimacy on the issue.

3. Choose Programs

The third section offers seven broad strategies for employing public diplomacy tools to promote religious freedom, including sample successful programs and more than 100 specific ideas for further implementation. The seven strategies, below, further strategic imperatives for public diplomacy:

- *Shape the Narrative*
  o Engage unexpected and credible voices in promoting religious freedom.
  o Employ creative media to increase awareness of and receptiveness to religious freedom issues.
  o Improve information available on religious freedom.
- *Expand and Strengthen People-to-People Trust*
  o Integrate religious freedom issues into traditional visitor and exchange programs.
  o Connect people of diverse religious backgrounds through multimedia.
- *Combat Violent Extremism*
  o Promote action-oriented projects that join religiously diverse youth.
  o Build long-term relationships through training and education.

The final section of the guide highlights recommended resources: recent books, reports, journals, articles, websites, blogs, videos and radio shows relevant to the American promotion of religious freedom abroad. Each reference includes a short description, most with hyperlinks to helpful data, background information and other materials.

DEFINE GOALS

U.S. policy mandates the promotion and protection of religious freedom around the world. With 70 percent of the world's population in countries with considerable restrictions on religion, that foreign policy imperative presents a daunting task.[42] A recent State Department International Religious Freedom Report acknowledged the challenge: "It cannot be stated categorically that any government fully respected [religious freedom] over the reporting year, even in the best of circumstances."[43]

Article 18 of the Universal Declaration of Human Rights defines religious freedom broadly: "Everyone has the right to freedom of thought, conscience and religion; this right includes freedom to change his religion or belief, and freedom, either alone or in community with others and in public or private, to manifest his religion or belief in teaching, practice, worship and observance."[44]

Clearly, religious freedom means more than reduction of religious persecution. The UDHR's larger vision requires social and political institutions that allow for true religious liberty, including a meaningful role for religious actors in public life. At the same time, religious freedom is often evaluated by only the absence of restrictions because the latter is more easily measured. Rather than simply citing violations in a particular country, an analysis of its restrictions can be a good starting place in creating a proactive agenda for religious freedom promotion. Because restrictions often reflect underlying social or political barriers to full religious freedom, a comprehensive assessment may prove vital in setting attainable objectives.

According to the International Religious Freedom Act of 1998 (IRFA), violations of religious freedom include:

- Arbitrary prohibitions on, restrictions of, or punishment for:
    - Assembling for peaceful religious activities such as worship, preaching, and prayer, including arbitrary registration requirements;
    - Speaking freely about one's religious beliefs;
    - Changing one's religious beliefs and affiliation;
    - Possessing and distributing religious literature, including Bibles;
    - Raising one's children in the religious teachings and practices of one's choice; or
- Any of the following acts if committed on account of an individual's religious belief or practice: detention, interrogation, imposition of an onerous financial penalty, forced labor, forced mass resettlement, imprisonment, forced religious conversion, beating, torture, mutilation, rape, enslavement, murder and execution.[45]

A helpful framework for categorizing restrictions on religious freedom has been developed by Brian Grim of the Pew Forum on Religion & Public Life. He outlines two types: government and social restrictions.

Government restrictions include: interference with religious practice, lack of intervention in cases of discrimination against religious groups, failure to provide constitutional or legal protection for religious freedom, limits on religious literature or broadcasting and favoritism of certain religious groups. Both policies and practice must be considered, as just a quarter of the governments in Grim's study fully enforced the rights their laws enshrined.[46] The IRF reports further identify five general government limits on religious freedom:

- Authoritarian governments' control over religious thought and expression;
- Hostility toward minorities, including intimidation and harassment;
- Failure to address societal intolerance or prevent attacks or other harmful acts;
- Institutionalized bias, such as laws or policies that favor majority religions; and
- Labels of certain religious or belief-based groups as illegitimate.[47]

These violations also span a continuum, the authors of *International Religious Freedom Advocacy* say. Religious persecution is the most extreme, followed by repression, in which religion is severely restricted, but not violently and systematically. Harassment, limitations and discrimination are progressively milder violations of religious freedom.[48]

Grim's second category, social restrictions, include: religion-related armed conflict, any violence motivated by religious hatred, religious groups' prevention of other religious groups' operation, harassment of women for violating religious dress codes and hostilities related to proselytizing or conversion. But a lack of social conflict does not necessarily demonstrate religious freedom; it may instead reflect government repression of public expression.[49] State officials may have many responses to social restrictions: lack of awareness, denial, indifference, shortsightedness or unwillingness to take responsibility. Each would require religious freedom advocates to take a different strategy.[50]

Grim finds that government and social restrictions tend to correlate, logical because religious freedom depends on the relationship between state and society, including how religion is approached in the public sphere.[51] However, there are exceptions to the link. In China and Uzbekistan, for example, where state authorities view religion as a threat, government restrictions exceed social ones. In Bangladesh and Ethiopia, where many citizens would like a particular religion to have a special role, social constraints are more severe than government restrictions.[52]

U.S. Government Promotion of Religious Freedom

In response to these varying attacks on freedom of religion, IRFA mandates that the U.S. government must promote religious **freedom and prevent any** restrictions on it by:

- Channeling security and development assistance to those states who do not violate this right;
- Working with other governments to develop multilateral approaches to religious freedom promotion;

- Using appropriate tools in the foreign policy apparatus, including diplomatic, political, commercial, charitable, educational, and cultural channels, to promote respect for religious freedom.[53]

To enable these efforts, IRFA established bureaucratic structures and processes. The law introduced the position of ambassador-at-large for religious freedom, created an Office for International Religious Freedom (IRF) in the State Department and established the United States Commission on International Religious Freedom (USCIRF).

Through the secretary of state, the president is required to designate "countries of particular concern" (CPCs): those that have committed or tolerated particularly egregious violations of religious freedom.[54] The secretary has a range of policy options for dealing with these countries, including sanctions, although in practice sanctions are rarely applied. A presidential waiver in IRFA specifies that actions need not be taken against a CPC if "the exercise of such waiver authority would further the purposes of this act."[55] Only one country—Eritrea—has had sanctions applied against it under this law.[56]

Instead the State Department's IRF office, led by the ambassador-at-large, typically works through bilateral and multilateral diplomacy to encourage reforms in CPCs. The IRF office, which is located within the Bureau of Democracy, Human Rights and Labor (DRL), also drafts strategic work plans to guide action on key countries of concern, and funds programs to foster respect for religious freedom. The office's "Annual Report on International Religious Freedom" covers 198 countries, describing the status of religious freedom, any policies that restrict religious practice, and U.S. efforts to promote religious freedom in each country.[57] Those activities may include official statements or meetings, interfaith workshops, grants for local projects that benefit religious minorities or exchange programs that describe the role of religion in the United States.

USCIRF is an independent, bipartisan federal entity responsible for making policy recommendations to the president, secretary of state and Congress. The president or federal legislators appoint nine commissioners, and the ambassador-at-large serves as a nonvoting member. Like the State Department's IRF office, the Commission monitors the status of religious freedom internationally and produces an annual report. Rather than cover nearly every country in the world, as the IRF report does, the Commission focuses on those it recommends be designated as CPCs[58] or placed on a Watch List for further monitoring.[59] The countries USCIRF recommends as CPCs do not always receive that status, as happened with Iraq, Nigeria, Pakistan, Turkmenistan and Vietnam in 2010.

In addition to analyzing conditions in particular countries, USCIRF reviews the U.S. response and makes policy recommendations to the executive and legislative branches of government.[60] Commissioners also conduct outreach on international religious freedom, visiting Congressional offices, convening and testifying at Congressional hearings, producing issue-specific reports, coordinating multilateral talks abroad and raising public awareness through media.[61] Some of the Commission's recent focal points have been religiously motivated extremist violence, defamation of religions, and asylum seekers and refugees.

In the decade since the IRF office and USCIRF were established, both have earned significant victories in promoting religious freedom. The reporting requirement has led Foreign Service Officers to make more local religious contacts and to examine countries' religious dynamics more closely, and U.S. pressure has persuaded some countries to free individual religious prisoners and to protect victims of religious persecution.[62] On a broader scale, several country cases have been noted as particular success stories for U.S. religious freedom policy. In Vietnam, for example, American officials and NGO leaders helped to negotiate the passage of a law that has reduced persecution, and in Saudi Arabia, the government agreed to push for textbook reform and to try to end funding that spreads Wahhabism.[63] In 2010, USCIRF counted among its accomplishments working to make possible a referendum on independence in South Sudan, and lobbying to lower support for a UN resolution "combating defamation of religions."[64]

Gaps in U.S. Government Policy

Despite these successes, structural and conceptual elements of IRFA have been criticized by experts outside and within government, including former heads of the IRF office.

According to law, an ambassador-at-large should report to the secretary of state, as this is a higher rank than an assistant secretary of state. In practice, the ambassador-at large for religious freedom reports to the assistant secretary for DRL, although other ambassadors-at-large report to under secretaries of state. The office's placement in DRL, some officials have said, distances religious freedom from the regional desks, preventing integration with other foreign policy goals. Because of this placement, religious freedom is often marginalized as merely a cultural or human rights issue, without attention to the broader security, political and economic implications of religion's relationship with the public square. A lack of dedicated funding for religious freedom within regional or functional bureaus limits broader attention to the issue. The IRF staff dedicates significant time to publishing the annual reports, and reporting work in the embassies is usually handled by junior political officers, with less attention from senior diplomats.

Conceptually, although the act refers broadly to advancing religious freedom, it established procedures focused less on promoting that right than on identifying problems and countering religious persecution. The original bill, the "Freedom from Religious Persecution Act," which was sponsored by Frank Wolf (R-VA) in the House and Arlen Specter (then R-PA) in the Senate, emphasized attention to religious persecution. Farr points out that "Ironically, neither Wolf-Specter nor (despite its title) the International Religious Freedom Act had as a major goal the promotion of religious freedom. Both focused primarily on identifying and reacting to the activities of persecuting governments."[65] The "least common denominator" of varying perspectives on religious freedom was to take a reactionary approach to humanitarian situations, rather than "implanting religious freedom as a cultural and political norm."[66]

Those reactive methods have sometimes been interpreted abroad as a "naming and shaming" approach to imposing American values on foreign societies. They have also been criticized within the U.S. government. One former State Department official has argued that such approaches to religious freedom promotion in China—lobbying for top-down discussions, for example, or pressuring the government with media exposure of detentions or arrests—have only short-term impact, while provoking anti-American sentiments, alienating allies and multinational businesses, and weakening American leverage in China.[67] Others have said that past methods have failed to address underlying causes. Farr, for example, calls the 2006 negotiation for the release of a Christian convert facing apostasy trial in Afghanistan a defeat for U.S. policy. He holds that the case ignored Afghanistan's failure to defend all citizens' right to full religious liberty, including Muslims' right to publicly debate the role of religion.[68]

In recent years, the State Department, supported by other government agencies, has moved toward proactive strategies to prevent violations of religious freedom, funding programs that engage institutions and societies in its protection. In 2011, the office had a $10 million budget to fund about 15 NGOs working with local partners to run programs promoting religious freedom. The projects included interfaith efforts, as well as training for lawyers, media and government officials.[69] Engagement on religious freedom has also become increasingly mainstreamed through the Office of Policy Planning, working together with the National Security Council.

A Public Diplomacy Approach

The tools of public diplomacy are key to furthering that new, soft-power strategy for religious freedom promotion.

In reaching beyond government elites, public diplomacy has a critical role to play in not only addressing restrictions but promoting the social conditions necessary for religious freedom. The Institute for Global Engagement has written convincingly on this point, in reference to its work in Vietnam:[70] "It's not just about top-down engagement to protect religious freedom, but also about bottom-up engagement to equip citizens to exercise their freedom responsibly."

Public diplomacy programs can help to:
- Reach citizens directly when bilateral efforts are not viable;
- Increase awareness of government restrictions, encouraging citizens to seek legal and political protections;
- Equip civil society to combat social hostilities;
- Promote a culture of religious freedom among younger generations;
- Publicize positive local developments for religious freedom.

Several current trends in public diplomacy—English-language training, private-sector engagement, an emphasis on youth and a focus on social media—present opportunities to promote religious freedom. Exchange and visitor programs, which one former under secretary for public diplomacy and public affairs called "the crown jewels of public diplomacy,"[71] are also natural tools for dispelling misperceptions and promoting dialogue, including among the American public. As sociologist José Casanova has argued: "The most effective long-term role for the U.S. in advancing religious freedom may be through its example as a society."[72]

In fact, some exchange programs have documented results relevant to promotion of religious freedom.[73] Through the Youth Exchange and Study (YES) Program, the Bureau of Educational and Cultural Affairs (ECA) has sponsored thousands of foreign high-school students for a year in the United States. Before the program, 10 percent of students felt confident in their ability to work closely with people different from themselves; 63 percent felt that way at the end of the year.[74] The proportion of students who said the right to practice any religion was "very important" increased notably, and participants also developed stronger beliefs in the importance of equal opportunities regardless of religion.[75] The majority of students said they had changed the opinions of others back home.[76]

As with other U.S. government efforts to promote religious freedom, the best public diplomacy initiatives will pursue context-specific objectives, helping to build social and political institutions to support that right. And the success of any public diplomacy effort will depend on many context-specific factors. Are appropriate partners engaged? Can relevant media, messaging and assessment tools be employed? How is U.S. involvement on the issue perceived? Government and popular perceptions of the United States deeply influence what types of programs are possible, whether high-profile U.S. affiliation is helpful and whether the American example should be highlighted.

Public diplomacy on this issue is likely to be effective where U.S. affiliation is an asset; elsewhere a high-profile U.S. role may raise suspicion or worse. In Egypt, for example, human-rights advocates have argued that diaspora-based advocacy for religious freedom, led by Egyptians in America, is seen as foreign influence and undermines the cause.[77] In Pakistan, the CEO of the largest television station was willing to take U.S. aid for education, but not for media programming on religious freedom.[78] And yet public diplomacy, for its capacity to reach citizens directly, remains one of a few viable options for promoting religious freedom in countries with uncooperative governments. In the most sensitive cases, exchange—for students, lawyers, journalists and scholars—may be among the most effective approaches.

What role the United States should play also depends on the specific issue at hand. In Bangladesh, where citizens largely view U.S. affiliation as positive, the U.S. ambassador can successfully raise awareness of religious freedom in general. But on the specific question of the country's minority Ahmadiyya population, whose approach to Islam many Muslims find controversial, responses to U.S. involvement have been mixed. Many mainstream Muslims in Bangladesh, including among younger generations, argue that U.S. officials should not consider Ahmadis Muslim, as that interferes with the definition of Islam.[79] The mainstream Muslims claim that U.S. diplomatic visits to Ahmadi mosques and attention to discrimination and violence against the Ahmadiyya community exacerbate the situation.

Of course perceptions of the United States are not static. Space for increased efforts can be created by effectively making the case for religious freedom and sufficiently addressing concerns about U.S. intentions related to religious freedom. Key cases and concerns are examined in the following section.

SHAPE MESSAGING

In applying public diplomacy to strengthen religious freedom internationally, context-appropriate messaging can help both to make a case for the right and to address any concerns about its promotion.

This section summarizes recent research and data in outlining four major reasons for promoting religious freedom, because it:
- Upholds an internationally recognized human right;
- Furthers national stability and international security;
- Contributes to economic development; and
- Advances democratization.

Following that is an overview of practical and theoretical arguments that address four common concerns about U.S. international religious freedom promotion. Those are that it:
- Defies the separation of church and state;
- Constitutes a form of cultural imperialism;
- Protects only Christians; and
- Overstates U.S legitimacy on the issue.

Making the Case for Religious Freedom

Religious freedom is both a fundamental good and an instrumental good, leading to other social benefits. Michael Posner, assistant secretary for democracy, human rights, and labor, writes that "Despite the varied conditions religious communities encounter around the globe, the principled and practical reasons for safeguarding their freedom remain the same: religious freedom is a fundamental right, a social good, a source of stability, and a key to international security."[80] Those reasons may have universal validity, but each factors more or less saliently in particular locations and situations. Familiarity with the range of reasons for promoting religious freedom therefore becomes critical.

Religious Freedom Upholds an Internationally Recognized Human Right.

> *"We believe that religious freedom is both a fundamental human right and an essential element to any stable, peaceful, thriving society."*
> *—Secretary of State Hillary Clinton, Remarks on the Release of the 2010 International Religious Freedom Report, November 17, 2010*

According to IRFA, the United States promotes religious freedom as an internationally recognized human right. All United Nations member states have voted to uphold it, and people around the world have responded overwhelmingly in polls that they want the freedom to practice their own religions. Commitments to "freedom of thought, conscience, and religion" are enshrined in international documents, including: Article 18 of the Universal Declaration of Human Rights (1948), Article 9 of the European Convention on Human Rights (1950, and subsequent Protocols), Article 18 of the

International Covenant on Civil and Political Rights (1976), and the Declaration on the Elimination of all Forms of Intolerance and Discrimination Based on Religion or Belief (1981).[81]

Various validations of human rights can be applied in making the case for religious freedom. The authors of the International Bill of Human Rights explained that human rights "derive from the inherent dignity of the human person."[82] As a human right, religious liberty can therefore be justified by a moral understanding of human nature, that existence implies a search for ultimate purpose. In *The Right to Be Wrong*, Kevin Seamus Hasson argues that the right to religious liberty stems from our status as "intelligent and free beings who are naturally able to know and to choose." He writes that "while our lives are our own, we naturally want to live them in community with others, expressing freely all that's important to us. The experience of these things is universal; it cuts across cultural boundaries."[83]

But human rights, religious freedom included, do not necessarily require a moral justification. They can also be supported by altruistic opposition to human suffering.[84] The modern understanding of international human rights is rooted in the atrocities of World War II, and like the UDHR, IRFA was drafted in part because of insufficient global attention to the suffering of certain groups. Human-rights advocates saw a lack of institutional response to religious persecution in, for example: Sudan, China, India, Saudi Arabia, Egypt, Iran, Iraq and Nigeria.[85]

U.S. policy on religious freedom has irrefutably helped to alleviate and prevent human suffering—through the release of prisoners, for example, and protection of vulnerable populations from state and societal hostilities. Still, much work remains in upholding this basic human right and preventing violations of it.

From 2000 to 2007, religious persecution occurred in every region of the world; in 86 percent of the 143 most populous countries, people reported being physically abused or displaced because of their religion.[86] Persecution was particularly pervasive in South Asia, with more than a thousand reported cases of violence, and the Middle East,[87] but it was evident almost everywhere.[88] And physical persecution was found to increase with government restrictions on religion. Moderate government constraints increased the highest level of persecution tenfold, and extreme state interference increased that level of persecution twentyfold.[89]

For both the individual and the community, the protection of religious freedom is particularly important because it forms the basis for many other rights. The scholar John Witte, Jr. posits that religious rights are the conceptual if not historical source of many others: "For the religious individual, the right to believe leads ineluctably to the rights to assemble, speak, worship, proselytize, educate, parent, travel, or to abstain from the same on the basis of one's beliefs. For the religious association, the right to exist invariably involves rights to corporate property, collective worship, organized charity, parochial education, freedom of press, and autonomy of governance."[90] Those linkages have been statistically corroborated. Researchers have found extremely strong correlations—

exceeding 0.6—between religious freedom and civil liberties, including press and political freedoms.[91]

Religious Freedom Furthers National Stability and International Security.

"We uphold our most cherished values not only because doing so is right, but because it strengthens our country and keeps us safe. Time and again, our values have been our best national security asset—in war and peace, in times of ease, and in eras of upheaval."
—*President Barack Obama, Remarks on National Security given at the National Archives, May 21, 2009*

Religious freedom not only holds moral and altruistic implications; it has positive, tangible social effects. In particular, it contributes to conflict prevention and resolution and is critical to national stability and international security.

Governments have frequently used national stability and the international war against terrorism as reasons to suppress religious groups. However, historical examples show repressive regimes claiming to maintain order actually spur radicalization. State restrictions have led to increased persecution and violence.[92] Limits on free thought and religious practice are statistically linked to instability, including in places of strategic relevance to the United States.

Restrictions on religious freedom typically correlate with various indicators of militarization and conflict, such as increased military spending as a share of GDP. Social constraints in particular tend to arise where there has been a recent armed conflict.[93] The likelihood of violence may depend on many factors, including the size of religious minorities, their geographic distribution, the history of conflict, external support and capacity for mobilization. It may also hinge on whether the relevant religious groups are internally divided or cohesive.[94]

In some of those cases, repression may predispose religious minorities to violence. Religious historian Philip Jenkins explains that persecution of those minorities can incite religious violence, even against the state, and may lead members of a religious minority to view themselves as fulfilling religiously sanctioned vengeance against their oppressors.[95] Scholar Ragnhild Nordås provides evidence that in countries divided along world religions, conflict is more likely when states have official religions and persecute religious minorities.[96]

Violence can result from not only repression of religious minorities but also restrictions on sects within a country's majority religion. When religious actors are not allowed an independent role in the public sphere, the result may be "pathological forms of religious politics," including religion-based terrorism and civil wars.[97] For example, as political regimes increasingly pressure nonviolent Islamists, they may withdraw from politics, leaving room for more-radical groups.[98] Uzbek government efforts to regulate Islam, for example, have led to increased Islamic militancy.[99] Saudi Arabia's forced integration of religion-state relations and failure to accommodate diversity within Islam "provided the seed-bed for the emergence of global jihadist terrorism."[100] Even if a government intends to target only violent elements of a religious group, there may be negative security implications. Threats to the group as a whole may "inadvertently elevate" the extremists."[101]

Religious freedom can enhance political stability by enabling moderate voices to counter extremist rhetoric. Grim cites an example from Japan in 1996, when the religious movement Aum Shinrikyo, seeing the government as a barrier to its vision, carried out a deadly gas attack on the Tokyo subway. The government responded not by limiting the group's freedoms—outlawing its observance, for example, or forcing it to disband—but by focusing on the perpetrators' crimes. That approach helped defuse the situation, and no further violence occurred.[102] At the same time, a healthy state relationship with religious minorities can aid security. In the United States, for example, "Muslim communities helped U.S. security officials to prevent over four out of every 10 Al-Qaeda plots threatening the United States since 9/11."[103]

Assistant Secretary of State Posner writes: "In an age when terrorist groups export their hatred around the world, religious freedom is critical to international security." Recognizing this link, U.S. national security officials have grown more interested in promoting religious freedom, alongside other human rights. The Pentagon now has an Office for Rule of Law and International Humanitarian Policy, and Joint Publication 1-05, "Religious Affairs in Joint Operations," explains chaplains' role in advising the joint force commander (JFC) on both religious affairs and the impact of religion on military operations.[104] That publication suggests questions to be included in a religious analysis, for example: the impact of media coverage of religious issues in a host nation and surrounding region; the level of repression of minority religious groups; and whether a U.S. and multinational presence in the area supports religious freedom or incites violence.[105]

Religious Freedom Contributes to Economic Development.

"In nations with powerful or significant religious communities (that is, most nations on earth), religious freedom seems to be the lynchpin. Without it, the other freedoms cannot do their work. When it is present, the result is more social capital and economic development."
—Thomas F. Farr, first director of the State Department's International Religious Freedom Office[106]

States and societies that restrict religious freedom tend to have low GDP's. The correlation holds for government and social regulation of religion, reflecting the importance of responding to both.[107]

Research also links religious freedom with a series of development indicators. The restriction of religious freedom is inversely related to the human development index, as well as health measures such as number of physicians, infant mortality rate and percentage of underweight children. Limits on religious freedom also show strong correlations with several indicators of low socioeconomic status of women. The number of seats held by women in national parliaments, for example, exhibits a strong inverse relationship with social regulation of religion.[108]

Religious and economic freedoms generally coexist.[109] The top 30 countries for economic freedom all scored high on religious freedom in 2007, and the worst 30 countries for economic freedom all ranked low on religious freedom. Similarly, states with notorious restrictions on religious freedom also show poor economic performance. The correlation reflects more than a general link between freedoms, because religious freedom scores measure dimensions beyond civil liberties.[110] China may seem to be an exception to the inverse relationship, but as the country develops economically, Grim notes, it is opening up and allowing more religious freedoms.[111]

Increased economic productivity relies on the entrepreneurship encouraged by religiously free societies, the international economist Theodore Malloch argues. Economic freedom and religious liberty value similar social traits, he writes, and "competition for religious activity creates healthy conditions for economic competition and activity."[112]

Religious freedom also lets religion thrive. Two sociologists of religion have described a dynamic market for religion, in which religious freedom allows "many organized faiths, each specializing in certain segments of the market."[113] Established state religions, on the other hand, have been found to decrease religiosity within a country, as measured by attendance of religious services.[114]

The positive effect of religious freedom on religion is economically relevant because evidence suggests that religion itself is good for development.[115] Religious and faith-based organizations generate significant social capital, increasingly considered as important to economic development as financial or human capital.[116] Studies have shown that religious beliefs and observance correlate positively with development indicators including health, well-being and life expectancy.[117] Citizens' religiosity may therefore increase a country's economic performance.[118]

Links between religious freedom and economic development are especially important to emphasize in countries like China, where many view religion as anti-modern.[119]

Religious Freedom Promotes Democratization.

"Freedom of religion and expression lead to a strong and vibrant civil society that only strengthens the state.... An enduring commitment to the rule of law is the only way to achieve the security that comes from justice for all people."
—President Barack Obama, Remarks to the Turkish Parliament, April 6, 2009

19

States that protect religious freedoms are more likely to be democratic and to guarantee other rights, such as free speech. Among the world's 25 most populous countries, six of the eight with the lowest government restrictions on religion are strong democracies. Seven of the ten countries with the highest government restrictions on religion have either no democracy or limited democratic practices.[120] Religious freedom correlates strongly with civil and political liberties, according to Freedom House indices.[121]

One possible reason for that correlation is that freely operating religion supports democracy by encouraging faith-based communities to engage in civil society and public life.[122] Religious freedom allows religious groups to employ religious arguments publicly toward common goods, and to strengthen civil society through religiously based education, charities and networks.[123] Because religious organizations often produce social capital in the form of "increased volunteerism, social commitment, integrity, and general creativity," writes the law professor W. Cole Durham, Jr., it would be "socially wasteful to regulate religion in ways that unnecessarily curtail its positive effects."[124]

One way to avoid that harmful regulation is by what the scholar Daniel Philpott calls "consensual differentiation" or "harmonious, overlapping autonomy between religion and state that works to the advantage of both."[125] Religious actors' pursuit of peaceful, democratic states rather than conflict-prone, authoritarian ones, Philpott suggests, is conditioned by their political theology and by the existing level of differentiation, or autonomy, between religion and state. While religious actors resisted democratization in 39 countries during the past generation, they promoted it in 70 countries.[126] And nondemocratic religious actors can become more democratic over time, he says, citing the Catholic Church as an example.[127]

Despite the relationship among consensual differentiation, religious tolerance and political stability, religious freedom does not require a separation of religion and state. USCIRF Commissioner Elizabeth Prodromou writes: "There is no single blueprint for an adequately liberal and pluralistic constitutional arrangement of state and religion. Therefore, the design of international religious freedom policies must work from the premise that there is a wide range of possibilities regarding the relationship between state and religion, as well as for the role of religion in public life."[128]

In Greece, the separation of church and state is not necessarily a critical element of democracy and its attendant religious freedom, the political scientist Alfred Stepan argues. After the establishment of democracy in Greece in 1974, he says, the key task was not disestablishment of the church. Democracy in fact required that "no constraints be put on the rights of Eastern Orthodox Christians to argue their case in the public arena."[129]

Allowing religious actors in the public arena is important for religious freedom—and for democracy. Just as repression of Islamic or other religious parties can have negative repercussions for security, it may also inhibit democratization. Those groups, if not for state repression, could be advocates for religious freedom and other civil liberties. As the scholar Emile Nakhleh notes: "Islamic political parties themselves—for example, AKP in

Turkey, PJD in Morocco, PAS in Malaysia, and PKS in Indonesia—once empowered from below, and now active participants in the political process, would begin to push for civil rights, gender equality, and, yes, religious freedom."[130]

Religious repression occurs even against members of the majority religion in very religious states, so long as debate and alternative viewpoints are not allowed in the public sphere. In Afghanistan, for example, Muslims have felt unsafe discussing women's rights and the execution of apostates, thereby giving courts full power to define Islam.[131] USCIRF Director of Policy and Research Knox Thames explains the challenge: "Politically moderate religious leaders are forced to the sideline through violence and intimidation, giving anti-government elements free reign to force their extremist religious views on the population. The result is a rising tide of violent religious extremism that could overwhelm the Afghan government in Kabul."[132] The Chicago Council Report cites not only Afghanistan, but Algeria, Egypt, Iran, Iraq, Pakistan and Saudi Arabia as countries where the exclusion of religious actors and parties has interfered with the development of democratic Islamic politics.[133]

Religious repression is not always violent. In recent decades in Bangladesh, the ruling Awami League has associated all Islamists with the anti-freedom fighters in the 1971 Liberation War. Many Bangladeshis have argued that, in fact, the Islamist party Jamaat Islam is among the most democratic and least corrupt of the country's political parties, and they have complained of the country's dogmatic, intolerant secularism. In that case, secular-religious dialogue among Muslims may be as necessary as building bridges between Muslims and members of minority religions.

The Chicago Council report makes the important point that no Islamist party elected to national parliament has tried to draw more on Sharia law for legislation; religious political parties often prove pragmatic.[134]

Addressing Key Concerns about Religious Freedom Promotion

Despite the many reasons to support and adopt religious freedom, Foreign Service Officers may still have their own concerns—or regularly encounter those of others. The following section gives an overview of recent research that responds to four major concerns about the U.S. promotion of religious freedom internationally. While some are misperceptions, others raise legitimate points that should be addressed and contextualized. In either case, public diplomacy can play a key role in addressing concerns about religious freedom policy both at home and abroad.

Religious Freedom Promotion Defies Separation of Church and State.

The separation of church and state in the United States is often misunderstood—at home and overseas. Some foreigners believe incorrectly that the separation reflects denial of or indifference to religion. Because secularism carries a strong negative connotation in many parts of the world, that perception can have serious consequences for international religious freedom promotion.[135]

In fact, secularism in the United States refers to a differentiation of spheres—autonomous yet overlapping—rather than a dismissal of religion.[136] Colonial Americans considered religion to have a proper place in the public realm,[137] and the First Amendment of the Constitution created a "constructive tension" between church and state, allowing dual allegiances to God and to government and encouraging moral arguments for the public good.[138] American religious freedom therefore comprises the freedoms of thought and action, as well as the right to employ religious commitments in the political sphere.[139]

Likewise, U.S. promotion of religious freedom abroad does not mean endorsement of antireligious attitudes. On the contrary, because religious freedom has a positive impact on religion itself, the policy helps to uphold religion. Perhaps relatedly, some U.S. government officials remain wary of promoting religious freedom. That apprehension is exacerbated by a lack of clarity and legal guidance on how the First Amendment's Establishment Clause applies overseas, including a misperception that the domestic separation of church and state limits America's ability to promote religious freedom abroad.

In applying the Establishment Clause domestically, state and federal courts use the "Lemon Test," which stipulates that any law must have a secular purpose, that its primary effect must neither advance nor inhibit religion, and that it must not foster "an excessive entanglement with religion."[140] Evolving jurisprudence has given greater latitude to faith-based groups,[141] but little case law exists regarding the Establishment Clause's extraterritorial application.[142]

One of the few pertinent decisions came in *Lamont v. Woods* (2d. Cir. 1991), in which American taxpayers sued the U.S. Agency for International Development for funding Jewish and Catholic schools abroad.[143] The court found that "the operation of the Establishment Clause strongly indicates that its restrictions should apply extraterritorially," but indicated that exceptions might be warranted for the purpose of national security.[144] Still, the ruling is not prescriptive. A study by the Center for Strategic and International Studies concluded that *Lamont v. Woods* provides insufficient direction for today's foreign policy issues.[145] It remains unclear under what circumstances exceptions might apply,[146] and USAID now says that it implements all of its programs abroad as if the Establishment Clause were applicable."[147]

When a recent audit found that USAID funds were used for the rehabilitation of Iraqi mosques and for HIV/AIDS education materials that included Biblical references, the agency's management responded by underscoring how difficult it is to distinguish between religious and social activities in societies where religion plays a central role.[148] Overall, the audit found that complex Establishment Clause issues required case-by-case review.[149] The U.S. Supreme Court has never ruled on the issue, and many factors suggest that further judicial pronouncements on this issue are unlikely.[150] Many experts have called for increased government guidance on the applicability of the Establishment Clause abroad,[151] and a new working group has been created to address that issue.

Legal uncertainty notwithstanding, the Establishment Clause in no way prohibits the promotion of religious freedom. In fact, that right aligns perfectly with the First Amendment's religion clauses, which ensure the free exercise of religion. As the Chicago Council Report notes, "the Establishment Clause reinforces religious freedom by ensuring that religion does not control government and that government does not distort religious preferences by subsidizing, preferring, endorsing, or favoring particular religions or religion in general."

A related concern is that America's promotion of religious freedom prioritizes it over other rights. Former Ambassador at Large for Religious Freedom John Hanford acknowledges that advancing religious freedom would be easier if the United States were more active in the international human rights community. He has argued, though, that IRFA, like much legislation, was sensibly drafted to focus on a single issue.[152] Special emphasis on religious freedom was necessary, says the religious freedom expert Jeremy Gunn, because the issue had been receiving insufficient attention. Special ambassadorships to deal with war crimes or Newly Independent States were similarly established to raise the profile of those issues.[153]

The perception of religion as a complicated, sensitive matter exacerbates general government wariness of engagement, and this caution may be costly for U.S. foreign policy. The United States must not avoid this critical global issue, but rather devote more attention to it and engage with it more deeply.

Religious Freedom Promotion Constitutes a Form of Cultural Imperialism.

Many Foreign Service Officers have encountered the impression that U.S. religious freedom policy is an attempt to impose American values on other societies.

While this concern may be exaggerated by leaders trying to deflect attention from their own abuses, it is clear that the United States adheres to and promotes particular values—at times unilaterally.[154] As the 2010 National Security Strategy (NSS) asserts, "The United States believes certain values are universal and will work to promote them worldwide."[155] Religious freedom is one of those values that the United States is willing to defend around the globe.

The NSS justifies promoting select values on the basis that "they have been claimed by people of every race, region, and religion" and that "most nations are parties to international agreements that recognize this commonality."[156] Like other fundamental human rights, religious freedom is widely sought and broadly valued. The Universal Declaration of Human Rights, which includes the right to religious freedom, applies to all United Nations member states; monitoring religious freedom holds governments accountable to that commitment.[157] Global populations polled predominantly want the right to practice their religion,[158] and most people in Muslim-majority countries both oppose government interference with religious practice and support free public debate on varying interpretations of their religion.[159]

Still, a desire to freely practice one's own religion is not necessarily accompanied by a belief that others should be able to do so, particularly when the other group's faith calls for proselytizing. The individual rights that define the Western notion of religious freedom are not always an easy fit with communal rights, including the protection of certain religious communities from outside persuasion.[160] As the scholar Winnifred F. Sullivan has noted: "In many places in the world, and, indeed, in parts of America…religion is communal. It's given, it's not chosen. It's public, it's not private. And it's enacted, embedded in the culture, not simply believed in a private way by an individual."[161] With this communitarian understanding of religion—a widespread view that is, in fact, older than the private understanding— proselytism can be seen as coercion and converting religions, moral weakness. [162]

The key question is how to draft a law that respects traditions that link religious identity not to choice but to "birth and caste, blood and soil, language and ethnicity," says law professor John Witte, Jr. "How does the state balance one community's right to exercise and expand its faith versus another person or community's right to be left alone to its own traditions?"[163]

International agreements explicitly recognize the rights of religious groups, as well as the right to manifest religion publicly. Article 18 of the 1966 International Covenant on Civil and Political Rights prohibits religious coercion, and Article 27 guarantees that religious minorities have the rights "to enjoy their own culture" and "to profess and practice their own religion." But, as Witte points out, Article 27 cannot "permanently insulate" religious groups from interaction with one another.[164] In a globalized world, communal rights must have limits, especially if a religious group threatens the life or wellbeing of an individual. The rights of majorities must be checked by the principle of equality under the law.[165]

The challenge of promoting religious freedom is "to invest in the creation of mature legal systems that protect the individual *and* organizational dimensions of religious expression," says the scholar Dennis R. Hoover.[166] "Respectful religious freedom," as José Casanova defines it, is "the product of a creative tension and balance between individual religious freedom and communal religious pluralism."[167]

Of course, views will still diverge. In the past decade, for example, countries from the Organization of the Islamic Conference (OIC) have promoted laws protecting certain beliefs and belief systems from defamation. But those laws, justified by religious tolerance, have stunted religious freedom and suppressed freedom of speech.[168] The laws have been used in Egypt and Pakistan, a USCIRF report notes, to imprison people who have called for political and religious reform. Protecting religions from defamation, the report says, "would suppress any discussion of truth claims about, among, or within religions—the peaceful sharing of which is an integral part of the freedom of religion or belief."[169]

The United States cannot support limits on free speech. Secretary of State Hillary Clinton made as much clear at a 2009 briefing. "The protection of speech about religion is particularly important, since persons of different faiths will inevitably hold divergent views on religious questions," she said. "These differences should be met with tolerance, not with the suppression of discourse."[170] Rather than ban speech that "defames" religions, the USCIRF 2010 Annual Report recommends that governments employ education, public diplomacy and law enforcement to counter religiously motivated violence or discrimination.[171]

Changing Perceptions Through Public Diplomacy and Improved Terminology

U.S. officials can support those efforts by acknowledging common concerns about the types of intolerance that often lead to hate crimes and social restrictions on religious freedom, but moving the focus from legal prohibitions against incitement to condemnation of religious hatred.[172] At the same time, officials can work through civil society, media, exchange and example, not only to convey positive messages about religious freedom but also to stimulate and shape debate.[173]

Public diplomacy can help dispel misperceptions that religious freedom policy imposes U.S. values abroad. In Pakistan, for example, repeal of a blasphemy law is unlikely if seen as the result of U.S. interference, argues the scholar Mumtaz Ahmad. Engagement with civil society and media, he says, is more likely to lead to change.[174] U.S. officials' formal pronouncements can be unwelcome, says Chris Seiple, president of the Institute for Global Engagement, and "the manner in which a message is conveyed is usually more important than the message when engaging a culture other than one's own."[175]

A shift in messaging requires a more nuanced understanding of terminology, beginning with the word "religion" itself. The modern concept of religion arose during the Enlightenment;[176] the term "world religions" was not used until the late 19th century in Western Europe. Modern Europeans saw religion "disappearing from their midst," the historian Tomoko Masuzawa explains, and the modern discourse on religion was from the beginning a discourse of secularization and "othering."[177]

The concept of religion is quite limited, some experts have argued, and its application can be problematic. Many people around the world have no equivalent term or category, argues the religious studies scholar Russell T. McCutcheon.[178] European and North American scholars, he says, have at times used certain types of Christianity and Islam as religious standards by which to judge other movements known as Christian or Muslim.[179] The religion scholar Wilfred Cantwell Smith has made the more pointed claim that "the term 'religious' designates those matters in Western history that have generally been called religious there—specifically, Christian and Jewish tradition and faith—plus anything else on earth that is significantly similar."[180] In the context of international religious freedom, the scholar Winnifred Fallers Sullivan has called religion too unstable a category for use in legal contexts.[181]

The evolution of the Western conception of religion and state has also defined parameters for religion in the public sphere. The modern state "required the forcible redefinition of religion as belief, and of religious belief, sentiment, and identity as personal matters that belong to the newly emerging space of private (as opposed to public) life," the anthropologist Talal Asad argues. Seeing the separation of religion and power as a modern Western norm, he argues that it cannot be applied in understanding Muslim traditions.[182]

Asad further makes the claim that all human rights are based on moral values, and that current universal human rights have a specific Christian history.[183] Muslims first encountered the Western conception of human rights not through the UDHR, the professor of Islamic law Khaled Abou El Fadl writes, but "as part of the 'White Man's Burden' or the 'civilizing mission' of the colonial era, and as part of the European natural law tradition, which was frequently exploited to justify imperialistic policies in the Muslim world."[184] Power leaves a legacy, the scholar Saba Mahmood adds, and contemporary religious freedom is "intimately tied to the history of European domination of the non-Western world, wherein the concern for religious minorities has served as a crucial argument and pretext for the exercise of European power."[185]

Those scholarly insights have practical manifestations. In Cairo, for instance, U.S. Embassy officials said they could see how their own beliefs influenced the way they promoted religious freedom. The American "cosmopolitan" view of religion, they said, was unlikely to be resonant in the Egyptian context.[186]

Other phrases may help address conceptual and definitional differences: "freedom of thought, conscience and religion,"[187] "freedom of religion or belief"[188] or "freedom of religion, protection to believe."[189] Phrases such as "freedom of thought" and "freedom of expression" acknowledge that restrictions on religion exist not only between majority and minority religions, but also within religious groups.[190] However, references only to freedom of belief or religious tolerance do not include the right to manifest belief publicly.[191]

U.S. terminology matters, but careful assessment of both local vocabulary and host-country frameworks around religious freedom may prove even more important. In some regions women's rights or citizenship rights are particularly powerful, relevant, concepts,[192] and religious freedom may benefit from being associated with such positive, resonant terms.[193] It is often possible to identify host-culture traditions and principles—whether based in national narratives or religious sources—that support religious freedom, and to ascertain the reasons for adopting religious freedom most salient in a particular place. Thomas Farr points out several examples of religious traditions' support for civil society and limited, constitutional government: "the Protestant work ethic, the Kuyperian concept of sphere sovereignty, the Roman Catholic commitment to religious liberty in

Dignitatis Humanae, general Christian principles of 'just war,' and Muslim principles of justice and charity."[194]

In the Islamic tradition, the religious studies professor Abdulaziz Sachedina has written about the "centrality of Koranic teachings about religious and cultural pluralism as a divinely ordained principle of peaceful coexistence among human societies."[195] U.S. Embassy officials in Cairo suggest that an emphasis on justice resonates with Egyptians, and scholars have written that credibility with the "Muslim street" in South Asia requires speaking about "*justice* (a concept which generally resonates more in the Muslim world than *freedom*) and emphasizing the importance of both religion and religious toleration in our own history."[196]

The scholar Maneeza Hossain suggests that "Malaysia's societal Islam, Islam Hadari, can be invoked as a form of Islam that accepts traditional cultural practices" and that religious freedom could be effectively promoted in Bangladesh by "a positive insistence on the future of Bangladesh as a state for all its citizens, with a recognition of the ancient and proven Islamic values of tolerance, diversity, and acceptance of others."[197] That locally relevant approach eschews inapplicable U.S. frameworks. Because many religious freedom issues in Bangladesh have to do with impunity for cases of violence against religious minorities, promoting religious freedom only as a democracy concern may ignore relevant issues.[198] In Europe, emphasis on the European Convention of Human Rights might be most effective; elsewhere UN charters may have more resonance.[199]

Successfully promoting religious freedom in East Asia may require emphasis on social harmony and stability, as well as equal rights for minority groups.[200] In China, efforts are more likely to be effective if they align with "growing domestic rights-consciousness and expectations for democratization under new leaders" and strive to "show these change agents that freedom of conscience, religion, and belief is not only morally right but also vital for developing a healthy and stable civil society."[201] That approach may cultivate positive views of religion—including its connection to economic development—to help religious freedom gain ground in China.

Religious Freedom Promotion Protects Only Christians.

Beyond cultural imperialism, some critics suggest that the primary agenda for U.S. religious freedom promotion is to protect Christian communities and new converts from persecution and to enable American Christians to proselytize abroad.

Interviewees in Egypt, for example, said they felt that religious freedom policy does not protect the average Muslim[202] and that it prioritizes the rights of minorities.[203] In Bangladesh, an NGO leader cited a perception that some Christian NGOs try to use the issue of religious freedom to gain support from the international community.[204]

Although U.S. religious freedom policy does not favor Christians over other religious groups, the roots of this concern are easily attributable to general perceptions of

27

American foreign policy. In many regions, religious missions are a primary source of contact with the West, and "occasional ill-considered, inappropriate, and unrepresentative behaviors by overzealous missioners" have influenced opinions of American intentions abroad.[205] Members of the U.S. military, who often interact directly with foreign populations, have also been identified with Christian images and activities, perhaps as a result of "the evangelical transformation of the military" in recent decades.[206]

Perceptions of bias in religious freedom promotion come in part from the way the policy developed. In the mid-1990s two groups advanced the religious freedom agenda in the United States: first, activists focused on preventing Christian persecution abroad; and second, a coalition of faith-based and human-rights groups that rallied around the issue more broadly.

The original bill introduced in 1997, the "Freedom from Religious Persecution Act," sought to establish a White House office devoted to victims of religious persecution, "especially (but not exclusively) members of the religious group [that advocates] argued was the most persecuted—Christians."[207] In defining "persecuted communities," the bill's "default focus was on Christians"; only two non-Christian groups were named. Some observers therefore concluded that the initial bill's purpose was to enable conversions to Christianity.[208]

Early attention to Christian persecution[209] reflected what was on U.S. officials' radar, and "persecution of Christians comes to the attention of the U.S. government more than other issues do."[210] The reports' coverage of religious freedom issues has become much more comprehensive in the past decade.

Still, Foreign Service Officers should acknowledge IRFA's origins—while also explaining that U.S. religious freedom policy has moved beyond the motivations of some original proponents.[211] The United States promotes religious freedom for all, regardless of religion or nationality. As USCIRF explains on its Web site, it has engaged with a diverse array of religious communities, including: "Uighur Muslims in China; Baha'is and Sufi Muslims in Iran; Ahmadis and Hindus in Pakistan and Indonesia; Muslims and Christians in India; Christians, Mandaeans, and Yazidis in Iraq; and Jews in Venezuela." Often communities are not even aware that the U.S. government is advocating on their behalf.

Officials do not prioritize Christians to the detriment of other groups. "The United States, in its bilateral discussions with other countries and in its public statements on this issue, never says anything like, 'Christians are particularly important,'" Jeremy Gunn writes. "The State Department stresses that it is not one religion or another religion that is at issue. It is the equal treatment of all religions."[212]

Discussing religious minorities' protections in the United States may help make the case that the United States is concerned not only about Christians' rights. For example, President Obama noted in his 2009 Cairo speech: "The U.S. government has gone to court to protect the right of women and girls to wear the hijab, and to punish those who would deny it." Government publications feature many documents illustrating the rights and inclusion of Muslims in U.S. society.[213]

A response to concerns about proselytism should stress that its protection upholds the freedom that all religious organizations need to thrive. Although proselytism can take coercive forms, the right to share religious convictions is central to the concept of religious freedom. Proselytism can be "an activity of peaceful persuasion, a staple of true religious pluralism, that is, creeds in competition within the umbrella of a democratic society committed to civility."[214]

Overall, emphasizing that religious freedom gives religious majorities the right to engage in the public sphere may help diminish perceptions that U.S. policy is concerned solely with protecting Christians. On a recent listening tour with young Arab civil society leaders, experts found that they objected to U.S. practices in promoting religious freedom. But far from demanding that those efforts cease, they called for the U.S. approach to expand—to promote political participation by religious individuals and to protect religious debate and institutional life.[215]

Religious Freedom Promotion Overstates U.S. Legitimacy on the Issue.

Critics at home and abroad have challenged the United States' legitimacy to lead on issues of religious freedom.

Certainly religious freedoms have been violated throughout U.S. history. One scholar argues that this history is not reflected in IRFA's wording, which instead "perpetuate[s] myths about American religious freedom."[216] She cites, to the contrary, the 19th-century Protestant establishment; persecution of the Mormon Church; systematic, government-promoted conversions to Christianity of Native Americans; and denial of religious rights to African-American slaves. Religious freedom in the United States also overlooks nonbelievers, she argues.[217] The 2009 IRF report notes that while Americans are rightfully proud that religious refugees have long found sanctuary in their country, the United States must also acknowledge its past mistreatment of minority groups, from Quakers in the 17th century to Muslim Americans after September 11, 2001.[218]

Lingering tensions over how to define and protect religious rights in the United States have flared in recent years, amid debate on the construction of an Islamic community center, Park51, near the site of Ground Zero in Manhattan. In response to widespread backlash against the planned center, the Park51 organizer Imam Feisal Abdul Rauf said, "I have learned that church and state are not always separated, even in America."[219] More recently, the Texas State Board of Education has considered a resolution to deal with perceived pro-Islamic bias in social studies textbooks, and some government representatives have pushed for hearings to investigate alleged radicalization of Muslim-Americans.

Religiously motivated hate crimes remain a problem in the United States, with the Federal Bureau of Investigation (FBI) finding them "in nearly all 50 states for every year in the 21st century," and recent statistics showing that almost 20 percent of all hate crimes—including murder, physical assaults and property destruction—were motivated by religious bias.[220] In 2004, the Council on American-Islamic Relations (CAIR) processed 1,522 reports of harassment, violence or discriminatory treatment against Muslims, an increase of 49 percent over the previous year and its highest caseload to date. Among the reports, 141 were actual or potential violent anti-Muslim hate crimes; many complaints concerned law-enforcement techniques.[221] CAIR's 2009 report shows a reduction in the number of hate crimes, but an increase in discrimination in the workplace and schools.[222] This has not gone unnoticed abroad. In the 2010 Draft Report of the Working Group on the Universal Periodic Review of the United States, a number of countries, including Egypt, Bangladesh, Qatar and Venezuela, call for the United States to decrease discrimination on the basis of religion or against ethnic minorities.[223]

The United States has neither fully prevented social restrictions on religious freedom nor enacted complete legal protections. One legal scholar points to Congress's limited success with statutes such as the Religious Freedom Restoration Act (RFRA) and Title VII of the Civil Rights Act, arguing that the laws' ambiguity allows for diverse judicial interpretations. For example, Title VII, which ostensibly requires employers not to discriminate on the basis of religion, is vague enough to "require employers to accommodate religion in nearly all circumstances, in some circumstances, or in no circumstances at all."

Although the United States lacks a perfect track record on religious freedom and a flawless model for export, its system allows open debate, acknowledgement of challenges and continuous improvement. The 2010 NSS recognizes as much. "America's influence comes not from perfection, but from our striving to overcome our imperfections," the report says. "The constant struggle to perfect our union is what makes the American story inspiring. That is why acknowledging our past shortcomings—and highlighting our efforts to remedy them—is a means of promoting our values."[224]

Throughout history Americans have learned from experiences of religious diversity. After the colonial-era theologian Roger Williams fled a theocracy in Massachusetts in 1636, he helped establish Rhode Island on a foundation of religious freedom.[225] When a 1940 Supreme Court ruling required Jehovah's Witness students in public school to pledge allegiance to the American flag, persecution of Jehovah's Witnesses followed. The Supreme Court then reversed its decision, and Justice Robert Jackson wrote "If there is any fixed star in our constitutional constellation, it is that no official, high or petty, can prescribe what shall be orthodox in politics, nationalism, religion or other matters of opinion."[226]

Efforts to protect religious freedom in the United States continue. In 2002 the Department of Justice strengthened enforcement by establishing a special counsel for religious discrimination in its civil-rights division.[227] In President Obama's speech in Cairo in

2009, he acknowledged that "rules on charitable giving have made it harder for Muslims to fulfill their religious obligation," and he pledged to work with American Muslims to ensure that they can fulfill *zakat*.[228] Gunn has noted "a dramatic change in the United States in the last 50 years on issues related to religion. Today there are relatively fewer attacks on minorities, and the United States should be very proud of that. But the important thing is that we acknowledge that we are promoting a universal standard, and that we be open to criticism by others."[229]

Admitting mistakes on religious freedom and speaking openly about failings can be an effective way for the United States to approach this issue. Government officials should avoid the tendency to compare American ideals to another country's realities, instead comparing actualities.

As public diplomacy shows how the United States has fallen short and how it has improved, it should also stress American success in building a society centered on religious freedom, one in which religion flourishes.[230] As the U.S. government reported to the UN High Commissioner for Human Rights in anticipation of the 2011 Universal Periodic Review: "Human rights—including the freedoms of speech, association, and religion—have empowered our people to be the engine of our progress."[231]

CHOOSE PROGRAMS

Public diplomacy programs driven by a country-specific goal, designed with appropriate messaging and guided by relevant concerns are most likely to promote religious freedom effectively.

This section offers seven broad strategies for employing public diplomacy to promote religious freedom, whether by cultivating respect for pluralism or raising awareness of rights. Each approach furthers at least one of three strategic imperatives for public diplomacy: shaping the narrative, expanding and strengthening people-to-people trust and combating violent extremism.

The description of each strategy includes sample successful programs and ideas for further implementation.[232] Of course any effective program must be context-specific, rooted in sophisticated audience analysis.[233] As one public affairs officer at the U.S. Embassy in Qatar explained, that country would be a difficult place to do programming related to proselytism, but audiences have been receptive to presentations on religion in the United States. Those talks have addressed misperceptions among Qatari youth that mosques are illegal in the United States and that American Muslims are constantly jailed; at the same time they have exposed participants to the American model of religious pluralism and perhaps fostered future openness to U.S. initiatives on related issues.[234] Each section's sample implementation ideas urge context-appropriate engagement with issues related to religious freedom, which might include gender equality, immigration and integration, citizen rights, human dignity and the rule of law.

The examples in this section include programs run or sponsored by the U.S. government, as well as projects supported by foreign governments or nongovernmental organizations. Some of the most innovative and successful efforts effectively use partnerships, beginning with intragovernmental coordination. Natural partners within the U.S. government include political officers active on human rights, USAID officials focused on democracy and governance and members of the IST team dedicated to countering extremism—all of whom may be leading efforts related to religious freedom that could benefit from a public diplomacy approach.

Outside the U.S. government, host governments and multilateral institutions can also be effective partners.[235] In Bangladesh, for example, some activists feel that European institutions have responded to human-rights issues more than American ones have.[236] At the same time, an official at the Dhaka-based British Council said she had never been approached by U.S. representatives.[237] Clearly, opportunities for increased engagement exist, and multilateral efforts can help define religious freedom as an international norm rather than an American value.[238] Partners may include local or U.S.-based organizations, companies, associations and religious groups or individuals. Comprehensive, searchable databases of religious leaders, interfaith groups and other NGOs active on these issues can be found through the Berkley Center for Religion, Peace and World Affairs at Georgetown University or The Pluralism Project at Harvard University.[239]

With a goal as broad as promoting religious freedom, evaluating success is vital, whether efforts target general populations, elites or future government leaders. Measurement should consider not only reach and engagement, but also credibility and impact,[240] including behavioral changes and not only attitudinal ones. Improved understanding and favorability matter, but ultimately success rests on diminished persecution and on the development of institutions that underlie religious freedom.[241] The most successful programs can be replicated or mined for lessons, and competitions can recognize and reward the best initiatives.

I. Shape the Narrative

The first strategic imperative of public diplomacy is to "develop proactive outreach strategies to inform, inspire, and persuade." This section will highlight programs that:

- Engage unexpected and credible voices in promoting religious freedom.
- Employ creative media to increase awareness of and receptiveness to religious freedom issues.
- Improve information available on religious freedom.

Engage unexpected and credible voices in promoting religious freedom.

An initial recommendation for shaping the narrative is to engage credible voices in promoting religious freedom, whether through language training, recruitment of diverse religious leaders or enlistment of unexpected actors to spread the message.

International dialogue on religious freedom can be stunted if scholars and religious leaders are unable to engage materials or express their views in a common language. Incorporating religious freedom into English-language training abroad has therefore become an important trend. Until recently, most English-language training was very general, but now materials and instructors are often chosen to convey certain values and to prompt discussion on particular issues.[242]

Since 2007, a U.S. Embassy-sponsored program has offered English-language instruction to faculty at Cairo's Al Azhar University, widely considered the center of Sunni Islamic learning, with 75 percent of its 400,000 students focusing on Islamic studies.[243] Enrollment in the two-year intensive English-language program has grown from 30 to 90, with rising interest each year. Participants meet three hours a day, four days a week for English instruction, and beyond that for workshops and other networking opportunities.[244] The program fosters faculty engagement in the international academic community, including in Islamic studies. In connection with the language instruction, the British Council offers a course, "English for Religious Purposes," in which participants give presentations on perceptions of Islam.[245]

The American University in Cairo hosts a similar program, but for clergy. Instructors combine general English instruction and Islamic studies with cultural exchange and discussion of values, encouraging imams to convey their own ideas in English. The class has analyzed, for example, a *Wall Street Journal* article by the Grand Mufti that condemned terrorism as un-Islamic.[246] Participating imams said the course altered their media-driven perceptions of Western hatred for Islam, equipping them to read Islamic-studies research in English and to express their own ideas on religious freedom.[247]

In Dhaka, the Language Proficiency Center, supported by the U.S. Embassy, has reached more than 400 madrassa teachers with courses intended to promote values through English literature. Instructors report that participants are motivated by common associations of English with modernity and development; they read classic American novels (chosen for maximum local resonance), watch films and documentaries, and listen to guest speakers on American culture.[248] The center has also conducted training sessions on social issues such as violence against women and child trafficking. Because 50 percent of Bangladesh's students are enrolled in the relatively inexpensive madrassa system, programs reaching its teachers have significant impact.

Another project in Bangladesh takes a different approach to engaging credible voices: empowering diverse religious leaders to tackle the issues of human rights and development. Religious leaders are poised to make substantial progress toward development goals in a country where more than one-third of the population lives in poverty and the government is ill-equipped to address national challenges alone.[249] Since 2004, the Asia Foundation and regional USAID partners have been engaging esteemed clergy through the Leaders of Influence (LOI) program.

In that program, imams from across Bangladesh participate in three-day seminars—conducted at the end of a longer Imam Training Academy—on human rights, public health, agriculture and education. The first day they meet with a local human-rights trainer; later they visit USAID projects, developing relationships that may extend far beyond the program. As of March of 2010, LOI had involved over 15,000 imams and made plans for the following year to reach a total of 20,000 leaders of diverse religious and secular backgrounds, including businessmen, elected officials, journalists, women, and young adults. Imams who have participated in the program report that they are better able to address social issues in their Friday sermons and more equipped to solve community problems such as interpersonal disputes and to address community needs by, for example, developing agricultural programs.[250] LOI also offers exchanges for leaders in Bangladesh and other South and Southeast Asian countries to share best practices. And the program hosted a major conference in March of 2010 on faith-based and community leaders' role in development, involving ministers, religious and civil-society leaders and senior U.S. officials throughout the region.

Uniting diverse religious leaders to discuss development or security issues related to religious freedom has become a common theme, including for Religions for Peace, a global organization led by senior clergy from around the world. In January 2010 in Jakarta, with support from the United States and Indonesian governments, the organization convened religious and civil-society leaders from those countries, as well as Cambodia, Japan, Malaysia, the Philippines, Sri Lanka and Thailand, to discuss strategies to fight poverty, promote religious diversity, advance good governance, and protect the environment.[251] Religions for Peace has also sponsored a program called Kedem: Voices for Religious Reconciliation, which, as featured in the USAID toolkit on religion, conflict and peacebuilding, has brought together Israeli Jewish, Muslim and Christian leaders to learn about one another's religions and plan activities for awareness and peace.[252] The first two years of the program focused on building trust among participants. In the second phase, participants began to carry out grassroots peacebuilding efforts—designing educational materials to counter inflammatory texts and a teachers' manual on each group's religious and national narratives, and trying to sway Israeli society through media outlets.[253]

Clergy Beyond Borders (CBB), an interfaith network promoting human rights, has also brought together Jewish, Christian and Muslim religious leaders. At a conference in December of 2009, clergy from the United States and abroad discussed human rights in their respective religious traditions. Together with the United States Institute of Peace and the Center for World Religions, Diplomacy, and Conflict Resolution at George Mason University, CBB conducts training in conflict resolution and peacebuilding, collecting case studies and proposals for publication.[254]

Not only can credible religious leaders help promote religious freedom, so can unexpected advocates. Too often, religious freedom proponents lack standing with their target audiences. For example, anti-Semitism, including Holocaust denial,[255] is increasing in some parts of the world, but figures who tend to speak out against such ideas rarely have credibility in those regions. Hannah Rosenthal, U.S. special envoy to monitor and combat anti-Semitism, has therefore attempted to enlist unusual suspects in her work.[256]

To that end, she helped lead a visit in August of 2010 to the sites of the former Dachau and Auschwitz concentration camps with eight Muslim-American imams and other religious leaders. The Muslim delegation reflected diverse backgrounds and included one imam who had formerly made a public statement denying the Holocaust. In a Congressional briefing, Rosenthal described the trip as groundbreaking. "As soon as the imams decided to pray by the Dachau sculpture commemorating the six million Jewish lives exterminated," she said, "I knew history was being made."[257] After visiting the sites, the Muslim leaders issued a joint statement denouncing anti-Semitism and Holocaust denial. "We condemn any attempts to deny this historical reality," they wrote, "and declare such denials or any justification of this tragedy as against the Islamic code of ethics."

The main objection Rosenthal heard about the trip was from members of the American Jewish community, who argued that some of the Muslim leaders who went should not have been engaged by U.S. government officials. Rosenthal and other leaders of the trip countered that such engagement was vital in dispelling misconceptions.[258]

Sample Implementation Ideas

- Employ English-language training to promote dialogue on religious freedom and related issues.

- Choose instructors and materials that convey the value of religious freedom and encourage related discussion.
- Target religion scholars, religious leaders and educators, introducing them to new perspectives and enabling them to express their own beliefs to an international audience.
- Offer professional development for participants through exchange with American scholars, religious leaders and human-rights lawyers. Encourage blogs and online discussions with U.S. counterparts working on religious freedom.
- Organize competitions to give top participants opportunities to use their new language skills in interviews with U.S. media or on speaking tours of the United States, either of which would expose American audiences to diverse religious perspectives.
- Invite American expatriates (e.g., private sector employees, students and tourists) of different religious backgrounds to serve as conversation partners, as appropriate.

- Empower diverse groups of religious leaders to further human rights.
  - Establish a committee of local religious leaders to advise on public diplomacy programs on religion and religious freedom.
  - Collaborate with those leaders to develop locally relevant terminology and activities, including pamphlets and online resources that discuss religious freedom—and the relationship between religion and the public sphere—from their own traditions. Use those documents to train educators and community leaders. Engage local clergy in identifying religious freedom issues that affect their communities (e.g., awareness of minority rights, prevention of religious tensions and interfaith cooperation on development goals).
  - Form interfaith committees—or groups of religious and secular civil-society leaders—to take on a range of development projects, such as election monitoring and health programs.
  - Publicize those leaders' efforts in the local media and encourage information sharing through personal networks, providing technical assistance. Give awards for outstanding contributions to religious freedom.[259]
  - Facilitate national, regional and international exchange among religious leaders, including through social networks. Connect local interfaith councils with American counterparts. Introduce religious leaders to individuals and organizations promoting religious freedom in-country, and make links with development workers and national security officials. If appropriate, connect local religious leaders with missionary representatives to establish joint principles or address any existing tensions.

- Enlist unexpected voices to spread the religious freedom message.

- o Find unusual suspects—particularly those with standing in a target audience—to promote religious freedom. Plan trips for unexpected advocates to visit sites of religious conflict or communities affected by religious persecution. Encourage press coverage of their experiences and reactions. In the United States, for example, a program bringing Jewish leaders to communities resistant to the construction of mosques could then release a statement from those leaders condemning Islamophobia.
- o Build relationships with influential members of majority religious groups, including those who do not frequently advocate for religious freedom and may be critical of U.S. policy, but broadly support human rights. Allow open dialogue on contentious issues such as defamation of religions and U.S. missteps in protecting religious freedom.
- o Organize campaigns—via television, radio, advertising, exhibits and conferences—that highlight the benefits of religious freedom for majority groups. Use locally resonant language to emphasize that religious freedom benefits religion.
- o Collaborate with private-sector representatives to connect religious freedom to business development or to host diversity trainings for employees. Facilitate partnerships, perhaps media campaigns, between companies and embassies to underscore the idea that religious freedom fosters the peace and stability in which business can flourish.
- o Collaborate with U.S. and local national security and military officials to promote the security benefits of religious freedom.
- o Build broad alliances to fight religious bigotry and persecution through exchange programs and social media. Connect American religious leaders and citizens of various religious backgrounds with communities abroad.[260]

Employ creative media to increase awareness of and receptiveness to religious freedom issues.

Some public diplomacy programs designed to shape the narrative on religious freedom have used creative media—film, television, music videos, novels, plays and visual arts—to break down biases and promote understanding, thereby increasing awareness of and receptiveness to religious freedom.

Many of those efforts qualify as "edutainment," which aims to both entertain and educate viewers.[261] Search for Common Ground (SFCG), which was founded in 1982 to foster peaceful relations between the United States and the Soviet Union, is a leader in the field. Today the organization works on conflict transformation and reconciliation in 23 countries; its media arm, Common Ground (CG) Productions, uses television, radio and other media to promote cooperation and peace.[262]

The Station, a CG Productions television series developed and written by Nigerians, follows a diverse group of characters, including reporters, cameramen and producers, as they attempt to cover incidents of violence in their neighborhoods. To do so they must set aside their ethnic and religious differences, try to understand one another's concerns and focus on a common desire for peace.[263] The program, which has been replicated in other countries, broaches serious social issues: police brutality, women's rights, government-controlled media, and public education. Notably, Egyptian state television banned only one episode of that country's version of the program, about relations between Muslims and Coptic Christians.[264] Another CG production, *The Team,* with versions in Morocco, Kenya, and Côte d'Ivoire, chronicles the struggles of soccer teammates from warring tribes, different genders and disparate socioeconomic backgrounds who learn that they must overcome their differences to play their best. The series is now in production for another dozen countries.

Other edutainment programs have opened communication between the United States and foreign audiences. For eight years the nonprofit Layalina Productions, Inc. has developed and produced Arabic- and English-language programming to license to satellite and cable television networks. Their shows, which tackle the most controversial issues in U.S.-Arab relations, reach tens of millions of viewers in primetime slots in the Middle East, North Africa and the United States. Layalina's flagship program, the reality travel series *On The Road to America*, follows four Arab college students on a road trip across the United States; it addresses stereotypes both of them and of Americans they meet along the way. The show was among the most-watched in the Arab world in 2007,[265] reaching 4.5 million viewers per episode. The following year U.S. stations aired it in primetime.

Egypt-based Video Cairo SAT (VCS) has produced a vast array of programs promoting democratic values and human rights. A recent show called *The Anti-Bin Laden* explores the life of Amr Khaled, a popular Egyptian Muslim televangelist, businessman and advocate for coexistence. Another VCS program, *The Bridge*, follows two Americans and two Egyptians as they develop deeper cultural understanding by participating in one another's daily lives. VCS has also run successful campaigns through text and video cellphone messages.[266]

Music can also be used to send a message of religious pluralism. The LibForAll Foundation, founded in 2003 by the Islam scholar C. Holland Taylor and former Indonesian president Kyai Haji Abdurrahman Wahid,[267] promotes a culture of liberty and tolerance within Islam. Its "Musical Jihad" program features Muslim pop celebrities in songs and music videos about Islam's embrace of pluralism. In Indonesia, the program has enjoyed particular success, thanks to the Southeast Asian pop icon Ahmad Dhani's song "Laskar Cinta," whose lyrics, inspired by the Qur'an and sayings of Muhammad, promote love over violence. Selling almost 7 million copies, the song was Indonesia's No. 1 hit in late 2005; a few months later it topped the charts of MTV Asia's program *Ampuh.* LibForAll plans to record the song in the language of Muslim listeners in every significant market (Arabic, Farsi, Turkish, Hindi/Urdu, Bengali, Swahili, Mandingue, Hausa, French, Spanish, Russian and English) and to host a major music festival celebrating Islam as a religion of love and tolerance.

Beyond television and music, other types of media have been effective in this work. The Face2Face Project in Israel and the Palestinian territories has posted side-by-side billboards of citizens from both societies. Emphasizing the physical commonalities between people of similar professions—teachers, taxi drivers and builders—can humanize foes, the project's creators say. The billboards have led to a book and a film documentary about the process of creating and posting the portraits. Another visual project, the U.S. government-sponsored "Mosques of America," has worked to change perceptions of Islam in America by illustrating the prominence and diversity of Muslim places of worship across the United States.

The diversity of a religious tradition might also be explored through poetry, as the New York-based non-profit City Lore, Inc. has done on global Islam, in partnership with Poets House and with funding from the National Endowment for the Humanities.[268] Through art exhibits, photography and literature, the British Council's Our Shared Europe Project hopes to address growing polarization between immigrant Muslims and non-Muslims in Europe. The project, intended to reach thousands of people in its first five years, aims to educate Europeans about Muslim life in Europe, including historic Muslim influence on European culture.[269]

Sample Implementation Ideas

- Partner with a private-sector firm, perhaps as part of a multilateral initiative, to cosponsor a film, television program or talk show that blends entertainment and social messaging to counter stereotypes and promote religious freedom.[270] Television programs, for example, that follow exchange between individuals from different religious backgrounds, or non-fiction documentaries that feature mutual understanding[271] help establish religious freedom as a cultural norm, in part by making discrimination and persecution seem socially unacceptable.
- Recognize and support media outlets that try to counter religious prejudice or highlight minority contributions to society. Set up live or online forums for likeminded media organizations to brainstorm future projects. Hold screenings to promote existing programming.
- Collaborate with private-sector firms or business schools to develop social marketing or advertising that humanizes minority groups who face social discrimination or religious actors who may be excluded from the public sphere.
- Partner with cultural icons who endorse religious freedom as not foreign but indigenous. Sponsor live or televised concerts to promote musical artists whose work advocates tolerance. Cultural programs, especially with well-known performers, may be particularly attractive to younger generations.[272]
- Support novelists and playwrights who espouse religious freedom. Develop, as Jennifer Bryson of the Islam and Civil Society Project describes, a nationally backed "Religious Freedom and the Arts program…to support development, translation, and distribution of creative media, such as plays and novels, that explore the role of religious freedom, and the social consequences of the lack thereof."[273]
- Encourage exchange, including social networking, among media, film, music and marketing professionals from societies facing a range of religious freedom challenges. Link these networks with religious freedom advocates.

Improve information available on religious freedom.

Accurate information is often lacking on both violations of religious freedom and the benefits of reducing them. Reliable data and context are necessary to improve interfaith understanding, alleviate tensions, and make the case to authorities.

U.S. broadcasting outlets and nonprofit organizations play a critical role in filling the information gap. America Abroad Media (AAM), founded in 2002 to help develop an informed global citizenry through independent journalism, works with leading reporters and broadcasters to create programming on critical international issues. AAM's hourlong radio documentaries and television programs air on prominent networks in Afghanistan, Indonesia, Pakistan and Turkey, reaching a total audience of 70 to 100 million. In April of 2010, AAM produced a radio show, "The First Freedom," on U.S. promotion of international religious freedom; it included in-depth interviews with U.S. and Pakistani officials, a case study of religious liberty advocacy in Vietnam and a discussion of how promotion of religious freedom in China fits in with other U.S. interests.[274] Another notable program, a radio discussion in 2007, focused on religion as a factor in conflict between the West and Muslim-majority countries.

Despite the importance of such programming, efforts to sow intolerance and undermine religious freedom often have significant resources backing their media and information campaigns. To broaden the scale of available information, programming can strengthen local media capacity to cover religious freedom issues. A U.S.-based program example to prevent misinformation about minorities is the Muslims on Screen & Television (MOST) resource, based on a partnership between Unity Productions Foundation and the Saban Center for Middle East Policy at the Brookings Institution, and in association with the Gallup Organization and the Muslim West Facts Project. MOST aims to provide the Hollywood community with resources and information about Muslims and majority-Muslim countries, both through facts and polls and through seminars and special events for entertainment executives.[275]

Training local reporters can also aid this effort. AAM, for example, runs a fellowship program that sends broadcast journalists from Muslim-majority countries to Washington for media and foreign policy workshops, as well as networking with American counterparts. The RelHarmony project in Albania, highlighted in the USAID toolkit on religion and conflict, also offers media training. The project has trained journalists and religious leaders to use media engagement, including televised discussions, to promote religious understanding. RelHarmony's staff monitor various media outlets' coverage of religious affairs and maintain databases of experts, leaders and institutions focused on both religion and conflict prevention in Albania.[276]

A particularly creative use of training and exchange to improve information on religious freedom comes from the Cairo-based Center for Arab-West Understanding (CAWU). Since 2004, CAWU has run a weekly electronic journal, the Arab-West Report (AWR), designed to improve Arab-West and Muslim-Christian relations through accurate reporting of religious discrimination and Muslim-Christian tensions. The Report summarizes Arabic newspaper articles in English and covers Muslim-Christian tensions in Egypt.[277] To produce the reports, Egyptian and Western interns travel together, often to rural Egypt, to research cases of religious discrimination. Student-reported articles may have limitations, but overall, the project collects important on-the-ground information and enables exchange between Egyptians and Westerners.

Sample Implementation Ideas

- Develop programming for U.S. broadcasting tools that examines not only religious freedom challenges, but also accomplishments. Encourage programs that explore religious freedom's relationship with both security and development, as well as different models of religion-state relations. Include discussion about the reasons for U.S. international religious freedom policy and U.S. efforts to protect religious freedom at home.
- Offer polls, facts and expertise on minority communities or other religious freedom-related issues to the broader, local entertainment community.
- Suggest locally relevant events or issues for local media outlets to cover. Develop databases of experts and institutions and propose interviews to enhance that coverage. Encourage local reporters to prepare their own profiles of cases covered in the IRF report, including feature stories on positive trends over time or interviews with survivors of religious persecution. As appropriate, give awards for outstanding coverage of religious freedom.
- Support projects that monitor media coverage of religious freedom. Respond to outlets that disseminate ideas counter to religious freedom or that misinterpret U.S. policy.
- Encourage or host media training, emphasizing ethics, to increase local journalists' capacity and willingness to explore religious freedom and objectively cover religious issues. Workshops need not focus exclusively on religious freedom; gender equality, immigration and rule of law, for example, are also germane.[278] Train journalists alongside religious leaders, as well as law-enforcement and government officials, to build relationships.
- Translate relevant books, reports and international documents into local languages. Increase access to printed and electronic materials on human rights and religious freedom, using radio, television and the Internet.
- Commission or publicize legal studies, economic research or children's books related to religious freedom.[279] Seek out studies on the impact of the news media on religious relations;[280] the root causes of sectarian tension; existing discriminatory legislation; and the statistical link between religious freedom and other social goods.[281]
- Run public campaigns, including digital outreach, to disseminate relevant publications.[282] Use them to develop curricula and teaching manuals, and make all materials available at American Corners, libraries, schools and other sites. Remember that illiteracy, censorship and poor distribution systems can inhibit dissemination, particularly on politically or religiously sensitive topics.[283]

- Offer technical and marketing assistance to NGOs investigating religious freedom issues. Support and publicize their work through online networks or international conferences.
- Highlight the social benefits of religious freedom, promote success stories and showcase minority contributions to society.[284] Publicize accomplishments locally and internationally.

II. Expand and Strengthen People-To-People Trust

The second strategic imperative calls on U.S. government officials to "build mutual trust and respect through expanded public diplomacy programs and platforms." This section highlights examples of engagement that:
- Integrate religious freedom issues into traditional visitor and exchange programs.
- Connect people of diverse religious backgrounds through multimedia.

Integrate religious freedom issues into traditional visitor and exchange programs.

One strategy to expand people-to-people trust is to integrate religious freedom issues into traditional, successful visitor and exchange programs.

Speaker programs have allowed religious and civil society leaders to discuss such issues. In the summer of 2010, for example, the U.S. Embassy in Canada hosted an International Information Programs (IIP) speaker to lead an interfaith workshop for new immigrants to the country. Relevant International Visitor Leadership Programs have covered topics such as "Religion and Citizenship in a Democratic Society" and "Empowering Minorities."

A particularly interesting exchange example is "Religious Pluralism in the United States," a program of the Study of the United States Institutes for Student Leaders. Funded by the State Department and organized by the Dialogue Institute at Temple University and the International Center for Contemporary Education, the first institute brought 20 student leaders from Egypt, Iraq and Lebanon to the United States for a month-long program to gain the skills and network necessary to advance religious freedom in their own countries.

The students explored New York, Philadelphia and Washington, D.C., learning about American history and contemporary society, with a special focus on religious diversity and pluralism. Participants visited historic sites, attended religious services, met with American students and spent a weekend with host families. As they examined the benefits and challenges of living side-by-side with people of various religious beliefs, their attitudes changed at the individual level—two students who initially refused to attend a Jewish worship service in Philadelphia were challenged by their peers to overcome stereotypes and go. Students from Afghanistan and Indonesia have participated in similar programs. Participants in such programs complete community-service projects, attend leadership-development workshops and develop action plans to advance religious freedom at home.[285]

The Islam and Civil Society Seminar, sponsored by Princeton University's Witherspoon Institute, also targets students, as well as professionals in Islam-related fields of study and work. In July of 2011, a weeklong program will bring together 20 to 30 graduate students and professionals from Bangladesh, China, Syria and Uzbekistan, among other countries, to discuss Muslim perspectives on faith and religious freedom, U.S. religious freedom policy at home and abroad and the relationship between religious freedom and development. The seminar will explore issues such as proselytization, apostasy and blasphemy.[286]

Specifically for academics and professionals, the Study of the United States Institutes for Scholars runs an Institute for Religious Pluralism, incorporating American history, politics and law. Hosted by the University of California at Santa Barbara (UCSB), the program invites professors, journalists and public servants from various regions—in the summer of 2010, 17 countries on four continents—to study American religious diversity.

Participants attend lectures by UCSB faculty on the history, law and sociology of religious pluralism in America. They visit religious institutions in Santa Barbara and tour cities around the country. At a free public symposium, they have an opportunity to speak to a local audience about religious diversity in their home countries. Alumni of the program have written papers and journal articles on their experiences; one Lebanese participant organized an Interreligious Academy in Beirut, bringing together Muslim, Christian and Druze students.[287]

Cultural exchange can also further religious freedom. The One World 2011 project, a people-to-people movement, plans to use cultural programming to counter stereotypes, including religious bias. In July of 2011 in Seattle, the project will begin hosting a series of multinational cultural and sporting events for Americans and representatives of Muslim-majority countries. The program will include an arts and culture festival featuring musicians, dancers and photographers. Another series of events will follow in 2013, in a Muslim-majority country.[288]

Sample Implementation Ideas

- Develop educational, professional and cultural exchanges; international visitor and speaker programs; and citizen dialogue initiatives to promote religious freedom. Organize programs around local reasons for protecting religious freedom or concerns about promoting it.
- Establish religious freedom as a broad social issue by bringing together religious leaders, economists, political scientists, other academics, legal scholars and lawyers, human-rights advocates, judges, journalists, cultural leaders and government and security officials. Introduce local professionals to regional and

- U.S. counterparts, building networks. Host local meetings before international conferences to cultivate locally rooted recommendations.
- Integrate religious freedom, subtly or more overtly, into any exchange program that involves religious societies—particularly those with restrictions on religion—or aims to improve understanding of American society.
- Draw on the expertise of religious American citizens and organizations on foreign cultures and religious principles.[289] Invite those religious leaders and citizens to participate in exchange programs.
- Broaden dialogue in host countries by involving American students, Peace Corps volunteers, humanitarian workers and other expatriates.[290] Develop an exchange program in which American youth serve as human-rights ambassadors, volunteering at related NGOs abroad.[291]
- Enlist U.S. military chaplains to help foreign militaries develop their own chaplaincies, using this as an opportunity to promote religious freedom.[292]
- Facilitate exchange among business leaders on hiring, diversity and religious freedom issues.
- Give exchange participants a platform to address the American public by organizing media interviews, funding dedicated publications and hosting symposia. Invite religious party leaders, including Islamists, to the United States to increase understanding of their parties and movements.[293]
- Work with participants to develop post-exchange action plans. Sponsor alumni competitions and offer technical assistance for blogs and documentaries about alumni experiences. Encourage alumni to develop programs in their own communities to bring together diverse religious and secular representatives. Use social networks to initiate follow-up discussions on related topics.
- Incorporate local ideas and frameworks from exchanges into future public diplomacy programs.

Connect people of diverse religious backgrounds through multimedia.

In addition to traditional exchange, some programs connect citizens of different religious backgrounds through multimedia tools that may have greater reach. Soliya's Connect Program, for example, which recently merged with the UN-established Alliance of Civilizations Media Fund, uses videoconferencing to link students from different countries and backgrounds, increasing cross-cultural awareness and understanding.

The program connects university students from the Middle East, North Africa, Europe and the United States for weekly, small-group discussions on religion, immigration, identity, foreign policy and the global economy.[294] Youth leaders facilitate the 10-week sessions, which progress from daily issues to more complex topics. Since 2003, more than 3,000 students from about 80 institutions in 25 countries have participated in the Connect Program.

Soliya provides a full academic curriculum for the program, which has been integrated into university courses in political science, media studies, English, sociology and communications. The program includes a media module in which students produce their own news reports with raw video footage from Al Jazeera and the Associated Press; their dissimilar products an opportunity to discuss media bias. Over five semesters, Soliya found that 93 percent of participants shared what they were learning with others in their community, and more than a third signed up for further engagement activities.[295]

A global British Council program has used similar technologies to connect clusters of schools in the United Kingdom and elsewhere in the world. Through the Connecting Classrooms program, schools collaborate internationally on curricula, and teachers and administrators join an online professional-development network. In Bangladesh, for example, the program has linked 90 schools with clusters of schools across the U.K., connecting more than 18,000 students in its first year. The network includes partnerships between madrassas and mainstream schools.[296]

Another youth-oriented project that uses multimedia to break down religious barriers is the Tony Blair Faith Foundation's Faith Shorts competition, which invites entrants under age 25 to submit short films exploring their feelings about faith.[297] The project provides equipment to aspiring candidates around the world who do not have access to it, ensuring that youth from resource-poor areas can still participate. Politicians, religious leaders and film critics judge the competition, and the winners' videos premiere at the British Academy of Film and Television Arts (BAFTA). In 2010, Faith Shorts received submissions from countries including Bosnia and Herzegovina, Egypt, New Zealand and Singapore.[298] Videos about individuals can resonate strongly with viewers and help to change perceptions. The Vienna-based Centropa project uses videos about the daily lives of Jews during the Holocaust, a format that could be used to help raise awareness about contemporary religious minorities.[299] Another digital program, the "This I Believe" project, compiles essays online—90,000 and counting—about people's beliefs, religious and otherwise.[300]

Several social media and networking sites also encourage religious dialogue, letting participants steer discussions. Among such sites are *Beyond Tolerance*, an online forum on theological and social issues, and *Patheos*, which features blogs and religion comparison charts. Another notable project, run by Odyssey Networks, a coalition of interfaith organizations that promotes social justice through media, provides spiritual videos for users to upload to smartphones and online pledges to pray for peace. *Altmuslim* offers articles, blogs, podcasts and a forum to explore topics related to Islam and gender.[301]

Many projects have employed existing social-networking sites to fight religious bigotry. For example, the 2011 Hours Against Hate campaign, launched by Hannah Rosenthal and Farah Pandith, the State Department's special representative to Muslim communities, uses Facebook to encourage youth to oppose all forms of social hatred.[302]

Sample Implementation Ideas

- Connect youth, clergy, scholars, lawyers, journalists and civil-society leaders through multimedia tools, including video sharing sites, social-networking sites and online forums. Link people of different religious backgrounds nationally, regionally or internationally, giving them a chance to express opinions, offer legal advice, share video or audio of sermons or worship services, and learn from one another. Connect religious institutions that are already using social media. Offer technical training to help marginalized religious communities find a voice online or survivors of religious persecution to make their stories known.
- Use general social-media sites to join individuals and communities of different religious backgrounds on social issues that may or may not include religious freedom. Moderate discussions to keep them on track, highlight key insights from participants, and follow up with off-line activities.[303]
- Employ videoconferencing technology to run workshops and symposia on religion and the public sphere, immigration and integration, foreign policy and human rights. Connect religious and secular schools from different communities, and train an international network of facilitators to lead online programs. Offer podcasts of U.S. university courses related to religious freedom and commission translations.
- Create local versions of international Web sites related to religious freedom. Use the professional networking site LinkedIn to connect clergy, educators and lawyers working on related issues globally. Host private Facebook discussions on relevant speeches or publications; upload town-hall meetings to YouTube. Publicize on Twitter interfaith efforts that raise awareness of religious freedom. Start wiki-style databases of likeminded individuals and organizations.
- Support social enterprises that develop locally relevant projects. Run a digital competition for young adults to submit films or other art about religion in their hometowns. Adapt for religious freedom the State Department's successful "What is Democracy?" video challenge, an annual competition in which anybody in the world may enter a one-minute video completing the sentence "Democracy is…"
- Engage Americans in these programs. U.S. Rep. Keith Ellison (D-MN) has proposed a campaign asking all Americans what they can do to carry out the vision from President Obama's Cairo speech.[304] Such campaigns can utilize Internet diplomacy to increase dialogue among citizens, communities and religious leaders in the United States and abroad.

III. COMBAT VIOLENT EXTREMISM

The third strategic imperative of public diplomacy is to "counter violent extremist voices, discredit and delegitimize al Qaeda, and empower local credible voices." This section highlights public diplomacy approaches that:
- Promote action-oriented projects that join religiously diverse youth.
- Build long-term relationships through training and education.

Promote action-oriented projects that join religiously diverse youth.

Some of the best examples of local, action-oriented projects come from youth programs. The U.S.-supported Bangladesh Youth Leadership Center, founded in 2008 by two Bangladeshi students, addresses social stratification as reflected in the country's split education system. The three-tiered system comprises private English-speaking, state-run and largely unregulated Madrassa schools, which tend to serve poorer populations.

The center's leadership training program, Building Bridges Through Leadership (BBLT), brings together students from diverse religious and economic backgrounds and all three types of schools. Many alumni have said that the program introduced them to students from different school systems for the first time and that they were surprised by how much they had in common. The center teaches leadership as a value and a skill, developing it in students through public speaking and group organizing. Groups of students also devise and implement community-service projects to address social problems. In the first cycle of the program, students worked in a nearby slum, focusing on disaster preparedness, sanitation, health and education. Several alumni of the program have founded notable service groups, including a social venture that gives female victims of acid attacks a chance to earn a living by making and selling handicrafts.[305]

A program at Columbia University also emphasizes social ventures, bringing interfaith youth leaders from the Middle East to brainstorm social entrepreneurship projects to promote peace in the region. The program, sponsored by Columbia Business School and Cambridge University, invites two dozen Jewish and Muslim social entrepreneurs from the United States, France and the United Kingdom to teach students both business techniques and religious and political history. For two weeks, participants work in groups to develop social entrepreneurship programs, pitching them to a mock executive board. Students see the network as a support system for future projects.[306]

Another U.S.-based program, the Interfaith Youth Core (IFYC) Fellows, observes that globalization and increased inter-religious interaction can at times lead to conflict, not cooperation. The program trains college students to lead interfaith efforts on college campuses, promoting understanding through action.[307] Since 2002, IFYC has worked with more than 150 campuses and trained thousands of young people in interfaith leadership; in October of 2010 the program led an Interfaith Leadership Institute hosted by the White House Office of Faith-Based and Neighborhood Partnerships.[308] Rather than political or theological discussion, IFYC training emphasizes action-oriented partnerships based on shared values. Fellows then promote mutual respect and religious pluralism on their campuses. A fellow at Yale University, for example, wrote a column in the *Yale Daily News* denouncing anti-Muslim sentiments after the shootings at Fort Hood in the fall of 2009.[309]

IFYC's resources for interfaith student leaders have included the "Better Together" toolkit, a guide for facilitating relationships and organizing action projects, and another toolkit on responding to anti-Muslim sentiments surrounding the proposed Park51 community center near Ground Zero. That toolkit encourages cooperation: "The 'Us vs. Them' is not Americans versus Muslims. It is Americans of all religious, non-religious and philosophical traditions united against violent extremism," it says. "We must proactively sustain interfaith engagement on campus by: incorporating religious and philosophical traditions into the standard framework for engaging diversity issues on campus; and equipping a broad range of campus leaders with basic religious literacy and an understanding of the value of religious pluralism in student life."[310] IFYC has also collaborated with the Tony Blair Faith Foundation's Tony Blair Faith Act Fellows, young people of different religious backgrounds working toward common causes not necessarily related to religion. In the first year of the fellowship, 2009-10, 30 fellows from the United States, United Kingdom and Canada focused on fighting global poverty and eradicating malaria.[311]

Another interesting example of youth activism, readily adaptable to religious freedom, is the British Council's International Climate Champions (ICC) program. Like religious freedom, climate change has local and international implications whose discussion is often dominated by elites. Since 2008, the ICC program has drawn thousands of young people from dozens of countries to join the conversation on climate change. Applicants submit project proposals and go through a rigorous interview process; those selected attend workshops and join an international peer network. The students' projects include plays, documentaries, cartoons, postcards and board games.[312]

A program highlight is the opportunity for some students to present their ideas to world leaders. In May of 2008 at the G8 Environment Ministers Meeting in Kobe, Japan, a select group of International Climate Champions called for an end to climate change. In December of 2009 at the UN Climate Change Conference in Copenhagen, 200 young people witnessed delegates' ideas for stopping climate change and presented their own.

Sample Implementation Ideas

- Promote programs that spread religious pluralism through action, fostering a culture that stigmatizes religious hatred and undermines violent extremism. Encourage local community-action programs for students of different backgrounds and fund competitions for interfaith projects on poverty, development and health. Absent a specific focus on religion, collaboration will still promote religious understanding.
- Establish leadership institutes for students from different religious and secular backgrounds, creating a prestigious training program on religious freedom. Simulate political models for students to explore how religious freedom can be protected at the state level. Cultivate post-program communication, as alumni may become key allies in reducing restrictions on religious freedom.
- Develop networks of youth activists to fight religious hatred, and invite them to propose creative multimedia projects to promote religious freedom, sharing their ideas through video clips on YouTube. Bring young people with bright ideas to present them at international conferences on human rights. Encourage young leaders to generate their own projects, which will be more rooted in local needs than would externally imposed programs, and provide them with appropriate training, connections and technical support.

- Support interfaith movements at foreign universities and link them with similar groups on U.S. campuses through online networks and videoconferences. Train interfaith activists in opinion writing and encourage them to submit columns to local publications.[313] Engage U.S. Interfaith Youth Core Fellows in exchange programs. Commission local organizations to create toolkits for student leaders on religious freedom and pluralism. Connect these youth leaders with networks for graduate students and young professionals involved in national security or development work.

Build long-term relationships through training and education.

Just as local initiatives can promote the benefits of religious freedom to help combat violent extremism, so can sustained, substantive training and education. Following short-term public diplomacy programs with NGO collaborations helps ensure long-term impact.

The Institute for Global Engagement (IGE), a faith-based organization in Arlington, Virginia, exemplifies that type of relationship building. One of the institute's most successful programs is in Vietnam, which was designated a Country of Particular Concern (CPC) in 2004 because "religious dissident leaders have been harassed, detained, and imprisoned and the Vietnamese government has continued its crackdown against religious minorities…including beatings and the forced renunciation of faith."[314] While that repression may not have led directly to violent extremism in Vietnam, similar state restrictions elsewhere have been linked to violent extremism, making IGE's approach here instructive.

IGE took a simultaneous top-down and bottom-up approach to promote religious freedom.[315] The institute's founder, Chris Seiple, employed what he calls "relational diplomacy," the "patient cultivation of respectful relationships and practical agreements to work toward religious freedom in ways that are consistent with the local culture and rule of law."[316] In February of 2006, IGE invited a delegation of Vietnamese religious and government leaders to Washington, where they met with U.S. officials and participated in an academic conference on religious freedom and U.S.-Vietnam relations sponsored by Georgetown and George Washington Universities.

The following June, U.S. academics and evangelical Protestant leaders traveled to Vietnam, and in September, IGE, several American universities and the Vietnamese Academy of Social Sciences hosted a conference on "Religion and the Rule of Law in Southeast Asia" in Hanoi. A delegation of American pastors attended the conference after visiting with religious leaders across Vietnam. By the end of the year, based in part on those efforts, the United States lifted Vietnam's CPC status; IGE continues to work with Vietnam on this issue.

IGE has since worked with the Vietnamese government's Committee for Religious Affairs to develop pilot seminars to train provincial authorities and religious leaders about the country's religious regulations.[317] The institute has also applied its concept of relational diplomacy elsewhere with considerable success. In Pakistan's North-West Frontier Province, IGE has partnered with Faith Friends, a local group including Sunni, Shia, Hindu, Christian and Sikh leaders, to promote interfaith cooperation. In Bannu, IGE runs a college scholarship program for both men and women, with intentional focus on religious freedom-related discussion.

Another program in Pakistan building long-term relationships that promote religious freedom is run by the International Center for Religion and Diplomacy (ICRD).[318] U.S. aid in Pakistan supports secular schools rather than the country's 20,000 madrassas, representing more than one million students. Those schools, about 15 percent of which preach violence or militancy, can also be part of the solution, says head of ICRD Douglas Johnston. He writes of "the untapped potential of the less militant madrassas to contribute to peacemaking if properly encouraged"[319] and argues for the use of "faith-based diplomacy" that brings personal belief into those conversations.

In the past six years ICRD has worked with more than 2,600 leaders of Pakistani madrassas and faculty from almost 1,500 of the schools, training teachers to promote critical thinking, to include scientific and social disciplines in their curricula and to emphasize religious tolerance and human rights from an Islamic perspective. The program provides a rare forum for madrassa leaders to discuss Islamic principles with members of other sects, and is one of the few madrassa programs to deal directly with human rights, democracy and interfaith dialogue.

According to an independent evaluation, 98 percent of participants said that as a result of the program they better understand the role of Islam in promoting religious tolerance and dialogue; 67 percent said they are including those themes in influential Friday sermons and other lectures.[320] Many said that their perceptions of other sects and religious communities have changed and that they have a better understanding of the West and the United States.[321] Some participants shared with evaluators that after ICRD training, they "stopped referring to the other sects as *zallin* [those who went astray]."[322]

Johnston attributes the program's success to its emphasis on madrassa leaders' own heritage of tolerance: the pioneering role of madrassas in the arts, sciences and promotion of pluralism a millennium ago. That approach has helped foster religious freedom in concrete ways. One madrassa partner, for example, organized a delegation of religious leaders to advocate for the release of 21 Korean Christian hostages of the Afghan Taliban in the summer of 2007. The following year another madrassa partner persuaded workshop participants that jihad in Kashmir was not religiously sanctioned.[323]

A program for madrassa students, the Legal Education (or Street Law) Program—included in the USAID toolkit on religion, conflict and peacebuilding—addresses discrimination against observant Muslims in Central Asia. The program instructs madrassa students in basic rights to decrease their receptiveness to extremism and promote the rule of law. Volunteer instructors at four Street Law Centers teach religious rights, gender rights, pluralist principles, social norms, and constitutional and criminal law. Students have said that the information enables them to engage more fully in a secular society.[324]

Embassies also conduct training and sustained programs on religious freedom. After September 11, 2001, the U.S. Embassy in Paris began working with Muslim immigrant communities around the city, sponsoring urban-renewal projects, music festivals and conferences. More recently U.S. officials have helped organize seminars for minority politicians, coaching them in electoral strategy, fundraising and communications. The International Visitor Leadership Program (IVLP) has increased its minority participants, especially Muslims.[325]

Sample Implementation Ideas

- Employ the principles of relational diplomacy in building long-term relationships to promote religious freedom. Institutionalize public diplomacy efforts on religious freedom through local government agencies, NGOs and universities. Work with American NGOs to succeed public diplomacy programs with sustained, substantive efforts to foster bottom-up engagement.
- Conduct joint trainings for lawyers and law-enforcement agencies, and involve national security and law-enforcement officials in discussions on the security implications of restricting religious freedom. Train provincial authorities on religious regulations, connecting them with minority religious leaders as appropriate, and offering to help those leaders promote positive developments for religious freedom in local media outlets.
- Invite local religious leaders and security officials to conduct trainings for U.S. government representatives on local issues related to religious freedom.
- Offer technical assistance, including media and networking support, to local civil-society groups that work on human rights, conflict prevention and interfaith understanding. Invite proposals for projects to raise awareness of religious freedom issues. Commission and publicize local materials that articulate the link between religious repression and violent extremism.
- Partner with local NGOs on education reform to combat extremism in at-risk areas. Train law students to lead sessions at religious schools that inform religious minorities of their basic rights. Collaborate with nonprofit groups to design training resources and educational modules for foreign universities. Provide scholarships for law students to attend U.S. programs related to religion and law, requiring that they return home to help build their countries' legal systems.[326]
- Conduct regional trainings to develop broader perspectives. Host conferences for academics and religious leaders on religion and the rule of law. Convene meetings for clergy, government officials and civil-society leaders to discuss legal implications for minority religious groups.[327]
- Engage and advocate for Islamists and other religious conservatives, showing those groups that religious freedom protects their rights, in addition to minority rights. Also strive to improve the U.S. image among minority groups, in part by assisting minority politicians and providing education and job training to minority groups.

RECOMMENDED RESOURCES

While by no means comprehensive, this section highlights recent books, reports, journals, articles, websites, blogs, videos and radio shows relevant to U.S. international religious freedom promotion. Categories include:
I.   U.S. Government Engagement with Religion and Religious Freedom
II.   Data and Materials for Religious Freedom Promotion
III. Theoretical and Legal Background
IV.   Religion and Religious Freedom in the United States

I. U.S. Government Engagement With Religion and Religious Freedom

Abrams, Elliott, ed. The Influence of Faith: Religious Groups and American Foreign Policy. Lanham, Md.: Rowman & Littlefield Publishers, 2001. Published a few years after IRFA's establishment, this collection of essays examines the history of religious influence on U.S. foreign policy, focusing on U.S. government efforts to prevent religious persecution and some of the challenges of this policy. Particularly interesting is Allen D. Hertzke's discussion of the political sociology of the U.S. movement for international religious freedom. Other chapters focus on China and on political Islam.

Albright, Madeleine. The Mighty and the Almighty: Reflections on America, God, and World Affairs. New York: Harper Perennial, 2006. Former Secretary of State Madeleine Albright draws on her own experiences in government to make the case that diplomats must understand religion's important role in international affairs. Albright traces the history of U.S. government engagement with religion up to the influence of evangelicalism in the Bush Administration. In the second half of the book, she focuses more specifically on Islam and the Middle East, including discussion of how to confront al Qaeda.

Amr, Hady. "The Need to Communicate: How to Improve U.S. Public Diplomacy with the Muslim World." The Brookings Project on U.S. Policy Towards the Islamic World. The Saban Center for Middle East Policy at the Brookings Institution. January 2004. Hady Amr suggests engaging Muslim and Arab Americans in dialogue, expanding polls in the Middle East to understand reactions to U.S. policy, and tailoring diplomatic practices to the demands and challenges of specific countries. Amr offers a list of resources on improving public diplomacy skills and emphasizes collaboration with leaders in Muslim-majority countries to develop joint policies, rather than operating unilaterally.

Appleby, R. Scott, et al. "Engaging Religious Communities Abroad: A New Imperative for U.S. Foreign Policy." The Chicago Council on Global Affairs, August 27, 2010. This report of the Chicago Council on Global Affairs' expert Task Force on Religion and the Making of U.S. Foreign Policy provides a pragmatic framework for engaging with religion and religious communities abroad. The authors outline the ways in which religion has been important in international affairs and offer recommendations for building government capacity to engage, such as tapping into the expertise of military veterans and civilians returning from Iraq and Afghanistan. The report gives recommendations for effective engagement, including working at the public level and engaging even those religious political parties that may oppose U.S. foreign policy.

Farr, Thomas F. "Diplomacy in an Age of Faith: Religious Freedom and National Security." *Foreign Affairs*, March/April 2008. Thomas Farr, the former director of the State Department's Office of International Religious Freedom and current director of the Religion and U.S. Foreign Policy Program at Georgetown University, argues that for the sake of national security, international religious freedom must be a cornerstone of foreign policy. U.S. foreign policy must go beyond simply opposing religious persecution, instead considering religion as a force for stabilization and the promotion of democracy. In the Middle East—specifically Iraq, Iran, Saudi Arabia, Egypt and Pakistan—the current U.S. IRF policy has been seen as a form of unilateralism and cultural imperialism. Farr lays out specific guidelines for how religious freedom efforts should be modified and articulated in each of these countries, emphasizing that support for dictatorial regimes is not a viable long-term solution for ending Islamic extremism.

Farr, Thomas F. World of Faith and Freedom: Why International Religious Liberty is Vital to American National Security. New York: Oxford University Press, 2008. Farr offers his insider take on the importance of fostering religious liberty and the U.S. government's track record on this issue to date. The book's introduction outlines the link between religious freedom and national security through a discussion of the apostasy case of Afghan Abdul Rahman. Farr also gives useful background on why both a classical realist and liberal internationalist approach to diplomacy may fail to lead to full engagement with religious dynamics, as well as a comprehensive history of U.S. international religious freedom policy. The book's final section offers principles for diplomatic engagement on religious freedom in the Middle East and China.

Farr, Thomas F. and Dennis R. Hoover. "The Future of U.S. International Religious Freedom Policy: Recommendations for the Obama Administration." The Institute for Global Engagement, March 18, 2009. On the 10-year anniversary of the International Religious Freedom Act, Farr and Hoover call for better integration of religious freedom with other foreign policy objectives. They outline ways for government to link religious freedom with democracy and civil society promotion, public diplomacy, counterterrorism policy and multilateral engagement and international law. Their public diplomacy recommendations include training public diplomacy officials on relevant theological principles within various religious traditions, and seeking the counsel of religious individuals and NGOs with experience in target cultures.

Hertzke, Allen. Freeing God's Children. Lanham, MD: Rowman & Littlefield, 2004. Allen Hertzke of the University of Oklahoma describes the rise of the faith-based movement for global human rights, showing how what started as an international movement to protect Christians from religious persecution has since developed into a larger movement to defend human rights. Hertzke presents case studies that illustrate the unexpected alliances formed by diverse religious groups to support human rights and fight religious persecution, at the same time shaping American foreign policy.

Johnston, Douglas and Cynthia Sampson, eds. Religion, The Missing Dimension of Statecraft. New York: Oxford University Press, 1994. This seminal work made the case that Washington must pay attention to the role of religion in international affairs. Senior scholars explored key case studies, including religious reconciliation in Nicaragua and the role of the Churches in apartheid South Africa. Stanton Burnett's chapter on the implications of global religious dynamics for the foreign policy community laid the groundwork for more than a decade of discussion on U.S. government engagement with religious factors.

Johnston, Douglas, ed. *Faith-Based Diplomacy: Trumping Realpolitik.* New York: Oxford University Press, 2008. Douglas Johnston argues for the use of "faith-based diplomacy," the inclusion of religious issues and concerns in global politics. Johnston notes that the radical secularism of diplomacy in the name of separation of church and state benefits nobody, especially because religious concerns are often deeply entrenched in ethnic conflict. Understanding the way religious actors affect global events is essential for preventing future violence. Johnston examines several contemporary case studies in which religious tenets could be applied in the name of peacemaking.

Johnston, Douglas M., *Religion, Terror, and Error: U.S. Foreign Policy and the Challenge of Spiritual Engagement* (Westport, CT: Praeger Publishers, 2011). In his most recent book, Johnston offers a practical blueprint for implementing his concept of faith-based diplomacy. He outlines a new framework for "spiritual engagement" as a guide to U.S. action abroad, and offers specific ideas such as improved engagement of military chaplains and faith-based NGOS, and assigning of Religion Attachés to certain embassies abroad. A particularly useful chapter considers the operational implications of church/state separation, calling for the president to task the Department of Justice to provide the legal case for religious engagement as a part of U.S. foreign policy.

Marshall, Jennifer A. and Thomas F. Farr. "Public Diplomacy in an Age of Faith." in *Toward a New Public Diplomacy: Redirecting U.S. Foreign Policy.* Philip Seib, ed. New York: Palgrave MacMillan, 2009. Jennifer Marshall and Thomas Farr underscore the importance of employing public diplomacy tools in promoting religious freedom. They argue that government officials' lack of emphasis on religion has led to "greater psychological distance" between Americans and the rest of the world, despite the fact that most Americans identify as religious. They prescribe a set of 10 approaches for including religion and religious freedom in public diplomacy, including effectively communicating the benefits of religious freedom to religious majorities and tapping religious traditions for principles that support civil society and limited, constitutional government.

Silk, Mark, Rosalind Hackett, and Dennis R. Hoover, eds. Religious Persecution as a U.S. Policy Issue. Hartford, CT: Greenberg Center for the Study of Religion in Public Life, 2000. In this edited transcript from a conference held one year after IRFA's establishment, participants debate issues related to U.S. international religious freedom policy. The conference, held at Trinity College's Center for the Study of Religion in Public Life, was notable for bringing together government officials, academics and human rights activists, and the debate held there reflects some of the fundamental theoretical and practical issues surrounding U.S. promotion of religious freedom.

"The First Freedom." **America Abroad Media.** April 2010. This hour-long radio show considers U.S. promotion of international religious freedom, beginning with an in-depth interview with a former director of State's IRF office. Pakistani officials are then interviewed about violence against members of minority religious groups. Two further segments look at the case study of religious liberty promotion in Vietnam, with interviews of both senior U.S. officials and relevant leaders in Vietnam. The program ends with a discussion of U.S. promotion of religious freedom in China, and consideration of how this goal is balanced with other U.S. interests.

The Review of Faith & International Affairs. *The Review of Faith & International Affairs* is a quarterly journal produced since 2003 by the Institute for Global Engagement, and published by Routledge Press. An issue titled "Religious Freedom and U.S. Foreign Policy" (summer 2008) is of particular relevance. Helpful articles include Jose Casanova's discussion on "Balancing Religious Freedom and Cultural Preservation," Asma Afsaruddin's "Making the Case for Religious Freedom within the Islamic Tradition," and Liu Peng's look at "Religion as a Factor in Sino-U.S. Relations."

Toft, Monica Duffy, Daniel Philpott, and Timothy Samuel Shah. *God's Century: Resurgent Religion and Global Politics.* New York: W.W. Norton & Company, 2011. The authors address the rising influence of religion and religious actors in global politics, arguing that religious actors have predominantly played a supportive role in recent global democratization. The book also includes case studies of the relationship between religious terrorism and the state in Northern Ireland, India, Sri Lanka, Israel and Saudi Arabia. The authors conclude with "ten rules for surviving God's century," including: "Learn to live with the fact that the issue is not whether, but when and how, religious actors will enter public life and shape political outcomes," and "Appreciate that there is strategic value in pursuing religious freedom in the conduct of foreign policy."

Government Resources

Annual Report on Religious Freedom in the World. **The United States Commission on International Religious Freedom.** The United States Commission on International Religious Freedom (USCIRF) releases an annual report on religious freedom abroad that summarizes the incidents or doctrines that have led to each country's inclusion in the report, recommending specific U.S. government responses in each case. The report includes sections on countries of particular concern, countries on the organization's watch list, and countries that have been closely monitored. The report offers separate chapters on how to engage with the United Nations and the Organization for Security and Cooperation in Europe in support of international religious freedom. USCIRF also occasionally publishes country-specific policy briefs.

International Religious Freedom Report. **The State Department.** The State Department's annual report, including information gathered by U.S. Foreign Service Officers around the world, describes the status of religious freedom by country, government policies violating religious freedom and U.S. policies to promote religious freedom. The report discusses both state-sponsored challenges to religious freedom and multilateral and regional challenges, and also includes a section on positive developments in international religious freedom.

"Religion, Conflict & Peacebuilding: An Introductory Guide." **United States Agency for International Development.** June 8, 2010. This toolkit from USAID's Office of Conflict Management and Mitigation stresses the important role that religious leaders and institutions may play in both conflict and peacemaking, identifying some of the challenges that government officials may face in partnering with them. The toolkit also presents case studies of USAID programs that have engaged with religious factors, outlining the lessons learned. While designed specifically for USAID personnel, the toolkit makes the case for any U.S. diplomat to work with religious actors, lending insight into related issues and addressing related legal issues.

II. Data And Materials For Religious Freedom Promotion

Barro, Robert J. "Spirit of Capitalism: Religion and Economic Development." *Harvard International Review*, Winter 2004. The religiosity of individuals in a particular country may increase that country's economic productivity, argues Harvard Economist Robert J. Barro. Barro shows that while religious service attendance links with a decline in economic growth, belief in reward and punishment leads to an increase in economic development. The article is based on research outlined in Robert J. Barro and Rachel M. McCleary's "Religion and Economic Growth," in the October 2003 issue of the *American Sociological Review*.

Berkley Center Knowledge Resources. **Berkley Center for Religion, Peace, & World Affairs.** Georgetown University's Berkley Center for Religion, Peace, & World Affairs offers a database of over 5,000 entries, including organizations, programs, publications, events, people, quotes and courses relevant to religion's relationship with politics, society and international affairs. Topics include engagement of religious communities abroad, inter-religious dialogue and new social media. Resources are also cross-listed by country and by religious tradition—such as Pope Paul VI's 1965 "Declaration on Religious Freedom". Two helpful resources are case studies of religious freedom issues in Afghanistan and Mexico. The Afghanistan case follows the lives of two Afghan citizens jailed for apostasy and blasphemy, while the Mexico case considers the lack of government response to hostilities against a growing Protestant population.

Education for Peace. **The Oslo Coalition.** The Education for Peace Web site is a resource for educators to use in promoting peace and tolerance. The Web site includes ideas for activities and lesson plans, including some specific to freedom of religion or belief. The educators who developed the site believe that knowledge about the other is only one component of tolerance education; students must also be taught the skill of tolerance. In one activity, called "Pictionary," an interfaith group of students are asked to draw whatever comes to mind when a particular religion is mentioned. The drawings done by the class are grouped together by religion and students are challenged to reflect upon what they and their classmates have drawn.

Institute for Global Engagement. IGE is a transparently faith-based organization based in Arlington, Virginia, that works to promote religious freedom globally through local partnerships. Their site offers international examples of their work in relational diplomacy and news updates on religious freedom. Of particular note is their collection of essays on "religion & security" and "engaging Islam" (which can be found on the homepage). Their Center on Faith & International Affairs has produced research in this field, including reports and links to a variety of syllabi for courses on religion and international affairs. Especially helpful for U.S. government officials are some of the religion- and region-specific articles published on the site. One author offers pieces on religious freedom and both Buddhism and Hinduism. Country-specific articles include "A New Framework for Promoting Religious Freedom in China," "Creating Religious and Cultural Space for Muslims in Southern Thailand," and "Religion in Europe: An Interview with Brent Nelson."

"Global Restrictions on Religion." Pew Forum on Religion and Public Life. December 2009. This Pew Forum report measures restrictions on religious freedom in 198 countries, covering the period from mid-2006 to mid-2008. The report finds that while both government and social restrictions on religious freedom are "high" or "very high" in only 32 percent of countries, these countries contain 70 percent of the world population. The Middle East and North Africa have the highest median score of both government restrictions and social hostilities, while China and India rank highly in each category respectively.

Grim, Brian J. and Roger Finke. "Religious Persecution in Cross-National Context: Clashing Civilizations or Regulated Religious Economies?" *American Sociological Review*. August 2007. This 143-country study offers statistical evidence that government and social attempts to restrict religious freedom are strongly linked to religious persecution. Brian J. Grim of the Pew Forum on Religion and Public Life uses the 2003 International Religious Freedom Report to develop tests by which to measure religious freedom and religious persecution.

Grim, Brian J. and Roger Finke. *The Price of Freedom Denied: Religious Persecution and Conflict in the 21st Century.* New York: Cambridge University Press, 2011. Grim and Finke provide their most comprehensive assessment of global religious freedom and persecution, analyzing data for nearly 200 countries. They also include case studies of Japan, Brazil, Nigeria, China, India and Iran, highlighting the diverse forms that religious persecution and religious freedom can take. The book reinforces the conclusions of the authors' earlier work: religious persecution comes at much too high a price for the governments and social bodies that enforce it.

"In Our Hands: International Religious Freedom." **First Freedom Center.** July 8, 2010. Created by the First Freedom Center, this video is a basic instructional tool for teaching about international religious freedom and the U.S. role in promoting it globally. The 15-minute video, which features interviews with experts and high school students alike, is accompanied by materials for the classroom, including discussion and essay questions, and links to other resources. The video encourages students to consider why religious freedom is an American value, whether and when the United States must intervene abroad to protect religious liberty—including how religious oppression is often bound up in larger ethnic conflicts—and how religious freedom affects individuals. Students are further encouraged to think about what they can do to promote religious freedom, both as individuals and as a group.

Marshall, Paul A. *Religious Freedom in the World*. Lanham, MD: Rowman & Littlefield, 2007. Paul Marshall ranks 101 countries and territories according to levels of religious freedom, based on measures of government regulation of religion, government favoritism of religion, and social regulation of religion. Marshall's report builds on the research of Brian Grim, whose 2006 "International Religion Indexes: Government Regulation, Government Favoritism, and Social Regulation of Religion" offered a social-scientific model for quantifying and comparing religious freedom across countries. The book also includes essays on relevant topics from experts in the field. In "God's Economy: Religious Freedom & Socio-Economic Wellbeing," Grim discusses the link between religious freedom and other social goods. And in "Free to Choose: Economics and Religion," Ted Malloch shows that religious freedom and economic freedom generally correspond, and that countries that do not encourage religious liberty tend to have a lower GDP's.

Pew Forum on Religion & Public Life. For almost a decade, the Pew Forum, a Pew Research Center project, has taken a nonpartisan, non-advocacy approach to promoting a deeper understanding of issues at the intersection of religion and public affairs. The site reviews the results of the Pew Forum's surveys, demographic analyses and statistical research on religion and public life, both in the United States and internationally. Within the United States, the Pew Forum offers graphics and statistics on the U.S. religious landscape, as well as covering public opinion on issues with a religious component, such as abortion or church-state issues. Globally, the Pew Forum conducts major public opinion surveys in addition to its work on government and social restrictions on religion, detailed elsewhere in this list.

"Report of the Georgetown Symposium on Religion, Democracy, and the Foreign Policy of the Obama Administration." Georgetown University, December 2009. This report summarizes the findings from a November 2009 Symposium on Religion and Democracy in the Foreign Policy of the Obama Administration, which included four panels related to religion and democracy. The first looked at the "twin tolerations" as a model for this relationship, while the second panel brought together academics who collect data on religion and democracy. Discussion on this panel considered the link between decreased social hostilities and differentiation between religious communities and government. The third panel considered the role of religion in U.S. democracy promotion efforts, while the final looked specifically at Islam and democracy. Also of interest is the report of a March 2010 Georgetown Symposium on Proselytism & Religious Freedom in the 21st Century that examines the political implications of proselytism and its legal and social dimensions.

Seiple, Robert A., ed. *Religion and Security: The New Nexus in International Relations.* Lanham, MD: Rowman & Littlefield, 2004. This edited volume provides essays on the relationship between religion and security, with attention to religious violence and repression, religious pluralism and stability, and religion and military intervention. In "The Politics of Persecuted Religious Minorities," Philip Jenkins argues that this type of persecution can create receptivity to religious violence, including against the state. Chris Seiple and Joshua White offer a case study of state repression of religion in "Uzbekistan and the Central Asian Crucible of Religion and Security." Christopher Hall and Osman bin Bakar consider the topic of pluralism and stability, from the Christian and Islamic perspectives, respectively. In "Pluralism and 'The People of the Book': An Islamic Faith Perspective," Bakar analyzes Qur'anic injunctions to outline an Islamic foundation for religious freedom.

Thames, H. Knox, Chris Seiple and Amy Rowe. *International Religious Freedom Advocacy: A Guide to Organizations, Law, and NGOs.* Waco, TX: Baylor University Press, 2009. From experts at the U.S. Commission on International Religious Freedom and the Institute for Global Engagement, this guide offers concrete tools for religious freedom advocacy, including an appendix with contact information for more than 100 non-governmental organizations focused on religious freedom (such as the Institute on Religion and Public Policy, Open Doors and Forum 18 News Service). The book includes a guide to organizations that protect religious freedom, including the United Nations, European Union, African Union, non-governmental organizations and others; a chapter is dedicated to U.S.-specific organizations. The authors describe the structures of these organizations and explain the commitments that each has made to religious freedom. The book also includes case studies outlining how religious freedom advocates worked to protect the right in Vietnam and Turkmenistan.

"Faith Diplomacy Initiative," University of Southern California (USC) Center on Public Diplomacy at the Annenberg School. USC's "Faith Diplomacy Initiative," launched in 2010, explores the intersection of religion and public diplomacy, with an emphasis on the global Islamic community and the role of religious organizations as public diplomats. The initiative has produced a special report on religion and global publics, a media monitor of headlines on faith diplomacy, and a bibliography of relevant books and articles.

III. Theoretical And Legal Background

Appleby, Scott R. *The Ambivalence of the Sacred: Religion, Violence and Reconciliation.* Lanham, MD: Rowman & Littlefield, 2000. In this foundational book on religion's role in international affairs, history professor Scott Appleby examines religion's potential both to motivate violence and inspire peace, making the case that both phenomena are spurred by the same dynamic. He also explains the concept of internal pluralism, that the major world religious traditions have lasted over time and in different geographic locations, leading to different schools of thought and religious orders within the traditions. In considering religious freedom and issues related to proselytizing, Appleby suggests that internal pluralism within religious traditions will allow people to embrace theologies aligned with international human rights.

Breistein, Ingunn F., Guro Almås, Sven Thore Kloster, Egil Lothe, and Dag Nygård. "Missionary Activities and Human Rights: Recommended Ground Rules for Missionary Activities." The Oslo Coalition, August 27, 2010. This Oslo Coalition pamphlet proposes guidelines for missionary behavior, and gives a succinct introduction to the issues surrounding missionaries and religious freedom, including suggestions for avoiding conflict. The document notes that both missionaries and those whom they seek to convert have at times been the victims of human rights violations, and therefore both must be aware of their rights and their obligations to protect the rights of others. The pamphlet suggests that missionaries must be careful not to "misrepresent or denigrate the faith of others," and that charity should be given without an injunction upon the recipient to accept the beliefs of the givers. Also of interest is the March 2009 issue of the *Review of Faith and International Affairs* on "Evangelism and the Persecuted Church," which looks at conversion and conflict, offering a number of Christian perspectives on proselytism.

Center for the Study of Law and Religion. The Center for the Study of Law and Religion has made 20 years of research on religion and human rights available to activists, public policy leaders, and media experts. A database of 430 publications considers questions at the intersection of religion and human rights from cases around the world.

Diamond, Larry, Marc A. Plattner, and Philip J. Costopoulos, eds. *World Religions and Democracy.* Baltimore: The Johns Hopkins University Press, 2005. In this edited volume, a number of high-profile scholars and leaders, including His Holiness the Dalai Lama, consider the relationship between religion and liberal democracy. Particularly worthwhile is the opening chapter entitled, "Religion, Democracy and the 'Twin Tolerations,'" in which Alfred Stepan explains his concept of differentiation but mutual respect between political officials and religious authorities. The following sections look at Eastern religions, Judaism and Christianity, and Islam, respectively. In "The Pioneering Protestants," scholars Robert D. Woodberry and Timothy S. Shah argue for a casual association between Protestantism and democracy, but show how that relationship is mediated by a number of other social factors.

Dionne Jr., E.J., Kayla M. Drogosz, and Jean Bethke Elshtain, eds. *Liberty and Power: A Dialogue on Religion and U.S. Foreign Policy in an Unjust World.* Washington, D.C.: Brookings Institution Press, 2004. This collection of essays from experts on politics and morality addresses whether religious ideals should influence foreign policy. Contributors including Michael Walzer, J. Bryan Hehir, and Shibley

Telhami examine the ways in which moral arguments are necessarily embedded in foreign policy decision-making.

Marshall, Paul, Lela Gilbert and Roberta Green-Ahmanson. *Blind Spot: When Journalists Don't Get Religion.* New York: Oxford University Press, 2008. The authors look at the media's relationship with religion, arguing that journalists often fail to properly account for religious factors. The book considers cases in which major media sources misjudge their approach to the religious dimension of a story, including misreading al Qaeda, misreporting on Iran and Iraq and underestimating religion's role in the 2004 presidential campaign.

Philpott, Daniel. "Explaining the Political Ambivalence of Religion." *American Political Science Review*, August 2007. This paper seeks to define the forces that lead some religions to promote democratization while others provoke political violence, offering some helpful case studies of both. Daniel Philpott of the Kroc Institute for International Peace Studies writes that two key factors can inform an understanding of that division. The first is differentiation, or the degree of autonomy between religion and state, and the second is political theology, or religion's doctrinal disposition toward the state. Ultimately, Philpott argues that the most stable relationship between religion and state occurs where there is religious freedom and a majority religion that supports a secular state.

Public Discourse: Ethics, Law and the Common Good. The goal of Princeton University's Witherspoon Institute's blog is "to enhance the public understanding of the moral foundations of free societies." The site offers regular postings on subjects related to law, morality and religion. Past topics have included "The Qur'anic Case Against Killing Apostates," "Did Pius VII Lie to Save Jews?" and "Political Responsibility and Exceptionless Moral Norms." Another worthwhile blog, specifically on issues related to Catholicism and law, is Mirror of Justice. Many posts relate to religious freedom, including articles about President Obama's views on same-sex marriage, the Supreme Court's ruling on the right to protest at military funerals, and the legal rights of parents to bring their children up in a particular religious tradition.

Stahnke, Tad and Robert C. Britt. "The Religion-State Relationship and the Right to Freedom of Religion or Belief: A Comparative Textual Analysis of the Constitutions of Predominantly Muslim Countries." U.S. Commission on International Religious Freedom. March 2005. This 2005 USCIRF report provides a comprehensive survey of constitutional language regarding religious freedom in 44 predominantly Muslim countries. The survey finds diverse expression of the relationship between church and state, religious freedom and related human rights. More than half the world's Muslim populations live in countries that have not declared Islam to be the state religion, and countries that have declared Islam as the state religion may have constitutional guarantees of religious freedom or belief in line with international standards.

Taylor, Paul M. *Freedom of Religion: UN and European Human Rights Law and Practice.* New York: Cambridge University Press, 2006. This study surveys the ways in which the United Nations and European systems protect freedom of thought, conscience and religion, and considers whether existing international standards on religious freedom are relevant to new types of violations. Also useful on the particular issue of religious registration in the Organization for Security & Cooperation in Europe (OSCE) region is Roadblock to Religious Liberty: Religious Registration (Diane Publishing Company, 2003), edited by Knox Thames and Ronald J. McNamara.

The Becket Fund for Religious Liberty. The Becket Fund is a Washington-based public interest law firm that works to protect free expression of all religious traditions in the United States and abroad, focusing on litigation, media and scholarship. Their site includes a blog covering international religious freedom news and country-specific reports that the Becket Fund has submitted to the United Nations Human Rights Council as part of their Universal Periodic Reviews of the human rights records of UN member states. Becket Fund lawyers have particular expertise in U.S. religious freedom law, but have also brought legal actions before international tribunals under international religious freedom laws. They have represented people from a broad range of religious traditions, and the site describes their litigation cases.

"The Dangerous Idea of Protecting Religions from 'Defamation': A Threat to Universal Human Rights Standards." U.S. Commission on International Religious Freedom. Fall 2010. This report from USCIRF demands an end to UN resolutions that prevent the defamation of religion. Those resolutions, sponsored by the Organization of the Islamic Conference (OIC), purport to protect religious freedom, while in fact they prevent free expression and give protection to state religions. The OIC has pointed to international standards that prevent hate speech and incitement to violence, but USCIRF makes clear that the language of such documents is purposefully limited so that it does encroach on the fundamental right of religious expression. The authors explain that preventing criticism of religion would protect religious institutions, whereas human rights organizations should be concerned with protecting individuals.

The Immanent Frame. Since 2007, the Social Science Research Council's Program on Religion and the Public Sphere has maintained this site, publishing multidisciplinary perspectives from both religious and secular voices on issues related to religion, spirituality and the public sphere. The site includes interviews and essays from leaders in the field, such as Harvey Cox, Reza Aslan and Karen Armstrong. It also hosts discussion boards on a variety of topics, including the politics of spirituality, rethinking secularism and religious freedom.

The Journal of Church and State. For over half a century, this academic journal has published research on the relationship between religion and the state. Published by Oxford University Press for Baylor University's J.M. Dawson Institute of Church-State Studies, the journal publishes constitutional, historical, philosophical, theological and sociological work, about both the United States and other countries. Each issue includes research articles and book reviews, including of books published in foreign languages.

The journal reports on global church-state developments and lists relevant, recent doctoral dissertations. It also occasionally publishes ecclesiastical documents, government legislation or court decisions.

The Journal of Inter-Religious Dialogue. This online journal is a forum for academic and social issues facing religious communities around the world, with the goal of increasing intellectual exchange between religious groups' leaders and scholars. Articles are peer-reviewed by a board of academics, theologians and non-profit leaders. The site also offers a feature in which graduate students, seminarians and young civil leaders respond to video interviews with religious leaders and thinkers.

Trigg, Roger. "Free to Believe? Religious Freedom in a Liberal Society." Theos, August 27, 2010. Roger Trigg, Emeritus Professor of Philosophy at the University of Warwick, argues that the concept of individual rights has Christian origins and that the separation of church and state does not keep religion out of political language and ideals. Trigg explains how secularization promotes contempt, rather than toleration, for religion, arguing that societies should recognize the religious roots of political freedoms, including religious freedom.

Williams, Rhys. H. "Religion as a Political Resource: Culture or Ideology?" *Journal for the Scientific Study of Religion*, 1996. Rhys Williams examines two common understandings of religion: religion as culture and religion as ideology. Those two lenses have often been considered either mutually exclusive or one and the same. Williams offers a more nuanced discussion of these two concepts, using examples to illustrate how the distinction can allow politicians to more easily utilize religion as a political resource.

IV. Religion and Religious Freedom in the United States

"A New Era of Partnerships: Report of Recommendations to the President." **President's Advisory Council on Faith-Based and Neighborhood Partnerships.** March 2010. In November 2009, President Obama created the Advisory Council on Faith-Based and Neighborhood Partnerships to oversee policies related to the service activities of faith-based and community organizations and to make recommendations to best support the work of those groups. The report includes a section on inter-religious cooperation, with recommendations to partner with faith communities to expand respect for religious freedom, and to build social cohesion by ensuring that Americans understand America's increasing religious diversity.

Faith in Public Life. This site considers contemporary news and issues related to the intersection of faith and politics in the United States. Launched in 2006, the site was intended to support a new movement led by religious leaders who wanted to promote "an inclusive and unifying faith movement advancing the common good in the public square." The site offers several online tools related to religion and politics, including a daily email with relevant stories, recent polls related to religion in America, and an interactive map of faith and justice-centered organizations throughout the country.

Especially interesting is an idea board of creative media campaigns run by faith-based organizations.

Hamburger, Philip. *Separation of Church and State.* Cambridge: Harvard University Press, 2002. Legal scholar Philip Hamburger suggests that insisting on a distinction between civil and religious society may do more harm than good. He gives insight into the complex forces that have shaped American separation of church and state, arguing that the First Amendment, originally intended to limit the power of government in religious affairs, has increasingly been used to confine religion to the private sphere via the concept of separation.

Hasson, Kevin Seamus. *The Right to be Wrong: Ending the Culture War over Religion in America.* San Francisco: Encounter Books, 2005. Kevin Seamus Hasson, founder of the Becket Fund for Religious Liberty, offers an introductory discussion on why religious freedom exists in the United States and the philosophical grounding for supporting it abroad. Through a series of stories, beginning with colonial and early American history, Hasson addresses the fundamental question of how a society can reconcile claims of absolute truth with human freedom in a pluralistic society. In doing so, he outlines the ongoing public debate between those who seek to publicize their view of the one true religion—whom he dubs the "Pilgrims"—and those who want to banish religion from public life altogether, whom he calls the "Park Rangers." He argues that the notion of religious freedom as a fundamental human right cannot come from a religious imperative, but rather originates in an understanding of human nature—the freedom to seek ultimate truth is necessary for human beings to be human. Individuals have the "right to be wrong" in their religious beliefs and in their search for truth.

Interfaith Voices. After September 11, 2001, Sister Maureen Fiedler started this weekly public radio program to promote religious harmony and interfaith understanding. For the past nine years, Interfaith Voices has explored national and international news related to religion. The show has covered anti-Muslim sentiment in the United States, religion and airport security, and the intersection of religious freedom and the U.S. military's "Don't Ask, Don't Tell" policy.

Khan, Muqtedar. *American Muslims: Bridging Faith & Freedom.* Beltsville, MD: Amana Publications, 2002. Khan considers different aspects of the American-Muslim identity, including the tension between American life and traditional understandings of Islamic values. The book includes a chapter on foreign policy, with a section on "Islam, Religious Freedom and U.S. Foreign Policy." Citing the foundations of compassion and tolerance in Islamic scholarship, Khan argues that American Muslims have much to offer both their own country and Muslims communities abroad.

The Pluralism Project: World Religions in America. **Harvard University.** This decade-long research project based at Harvard University aims to engage students in studying the new religious diversity in the United States, with particular attention to the communities and religious traditions of Asia and the Middle East that have become part of the American religious landscape. The project works to document American religious demography, study American religious communities, conduct case studies of pluralism in particular cities and towns and explore the challenges and opportunities of a public commitment to pluralism. The site offers On Common Ground: World Religions in America, a multimedia interactive CD-ROM with an introduction to America's new religious landscape, including exploring questions about American identity. The site also includes both domestic and international updates on news related to religious diversity.

Witte, John Jr. and Joel A. Nichols. *Religion and the American Constitutional Experiment: Third Edition.* Boulder: Westview Press, 2010. John Witte, Jr. of Emory University and Joel A. Nichols of the University of St. Thomas present an introduction to the history of religious freedom in the United States. The book traces the conceptual and legal history of religious liberty from the colonial period to today, with topics including government funding of religious schools, display of religious symbols on public property and the complex relationship between religious organizations and the law. The authors discuss the Supreme Court cases that have set the standards for these issues through their First Amendment interpretations.

Government Resources

All below can be found through America.gov.

"A Land called Paradise." The December 2007 video asks over 2,000 American Muslims what they would wish to say to the rest of the world. The video then shows images of American Muslims holding signs that reveal their personal responses—mundane and profound, humorous and serious. Also, "Diversity: American Ramadan," covers an event at Liberty Science Center that exhibits Muslim contributions to science. At the end of the video, the videographer asks Muslim attendees what they like best about being Muslim in America; interviewees reply that religious freedom allows them to practice Islam as they wish.

"A Multicultural Ramadan." This feature offers multimedia coverage of Ramadan in the United States and around the world, showcasing the freedom of American Muslims to practice their religion as well as the U.S. commitment to multiculturalism. It includes personal essays from four Muslim Americans, a video greeting from President Obama to Muslims on the occasion of Ramadan, and a photo gallery of Ramadan being observed worldwide. The feature also links to an article about the President hosting Iftar at the White House. America.gov also maintains Islam Around the World, a collection of over 1,800 user-submitted photos of Muslim life around the world.

"Being Muslim in America." This State Department publication illustrates how being a practicing Muslim and an American are not incompatible, and gives an introduction to Muslim life in the United States. The book opens with images of American Muslims engaged in everyday activities: grocery shopping, playing sports, working, praying, and spending time with family. These photos are followed by profiles of young Muslim Americans—an artist, an imam, a filmmaker, and a businessman. A "Statistical Portrait of Muslims in America" reveals, for example, that the largest group of American

Muslims is originally from South Asia and that nearly one-third of Muslim Americans live in the American South. The book includes short descriptions of mosques from around the country, and closes with a timeline of key events in the history of Muslims in America.

"**Birthplace of American Religious Freedom**." This feature offers an interactive case study of religious freedom in the United States, using the Flushing, Queens neighborhood of New York City as an example of both religious diversity and multiculturalism. A map on the front page pinpoints places of worship in Flushing, showing that Hindus, Buddhists, Muslims, Christians, Jews and Taoists all worship within blocks of each other. Part of the reason that Flushing has such a diverse religious makeup is that for centuries, the area has attracted new immigrants, not least because of a loophole in the zoning laws that made it easy to transform storefronts and homes into places of worship.

"**Freedom of Faith**." Published by the State Department in 2008, Freedom of Faith gives a basic introduction to the issues surrounding religious freedom in the United States, including historical roots and contemporary practice. The 36-page book features essays from scholars of religion, law, and American history. Among those scholars is Harvard Divinity School Professor Diana L. Eck, who emphasizes the dynamic nature of religious traditions, especially when people of different faith traditions encounter one another. Case studies related to separation of church and state are presented by Oklahoma City University Law Professor Law Andrew C. Spiropoulos, and Ambassador-at-Large for International Religious Freedom John Hanford describes the work of the Office of International Freedom at the State Department. Another section gives a summary of significant Supreme Court rulings on the Free Exercise Clause.

"**Talking Faith**." This America.gov blog, formerly run by State Department official Alexandra Abboud, covers current issues related to religion and the U.S. government for an international readership. Abboud often addressed topics related to religious freedom, including speeches given by government leaders and relevant developments at the United Nations. "Talking Faith" also hosted guest bloggers, including R. Gustav Niebuhr, a journalist and religion professor who presents religion in America as a microcosm of global religious diversity. While the blog is no longer regularly updated, it covers news on religion and America over the past two years.

"**Three Faiths Building Community**," and "**Walking to End Hunger**." These videos show recent interfaith efforts in Hartford, Connecticut. In the first, Muslims, Jews and Christians came together with Habitat for Humanity to build a house for a needy family. In the second, interfaith participants in the 25th Annual Walk Against Hunger describe the theological imperatives behind their decisions to be activists against hunger.

INTERVIEWEES

Alexandra Abboud
Staff Editor, Bureau of International Information Programs, U.S. Department of State

Sana Abed-Kotob
Chief of Regional Programs Division, International Visitors Office, U.S. Department of State

Ejaj Ahmed
President, Bangladesh Youth Leadership Center

Firoze Ahmed
Political Specialist, U.S. Embassy, Bangladesh

Syed Nazrul Ahsan
Teacher Trainer and Senior Teacher, Language Proficiency Center

Sehreen Noor Ali
Strategic Planning Officer for Public Diplomacy, U.S. Department of State

Matt Armstrong
Founder and President, The MountainRunner Institute

David P. Arulanantham
Political Officer, U.S. Embassy, Bangladesh

Karim Awadallah
Staff, U.S. Embassy, Egypt

Hossam Baghat
Executive Director, Egyptian Initiative for Personal Rights

Dwight Bashir
Deputy Director for Policy and Research, USCIRF

Brent Beemer
Division Chief, Office of Citizen Exchanges, U.S. Department of State

Judd Birdsall
Special Assistant to the Director of Policy Planning, U.S. Department of State

Harry Blair
Professor of Political Science, Duke University

Jodi Breisler

Assistant Information Officer, U.S. Embassy, Greece

Jessica Brown
Public Affairs, U.S. Department of State

Jennifer Bryson
Director of the Islam and Civil Society Project, Witherspoon Institute

Brian E. Carlson
Senior Liaison for Strategic Communication for the Under Secretary for Public Diplomacy and Public Affairs, U.S. Department of State

Mark Carlson
Office of International Religious Freedom, Bureau of Democracy, Human Rights and Labor, U.S. Department of State

Ahmad Tabshir Choudhury
Member, National Executive Committee
Coordinator, Public Relations & External Affairs

Warren Cofsky
Foreign Affairs Officer, Bureau of Democracy, Human Rights and Labor, U.S. Department of State

Catherine Cosman
Senior Policy Analyst, USCIRF

Paulinus Costa
Archbishop of Bangladesh

Rosaline Costa
Human Rights Advocate and Coordinator, Hotline Human Rights Bangladesh

Michael Cromartie
Vice President, Ethics and Public Policy Center

Louis J. D'Amore
Founder and President, International Institute for Peace through Tourism

Dennis D. Datta
Consultant, Koinonia

Sukla Dey
Program Coordinator, Books for Asia Program, The Asia Foundation

Aroma Dutta

Executive Director, PRIP Trust

Mona Makram Ebiad
Egyptian Politician

Shereef Mohammed Edreis
Cairo-based Imam

Taskin Fahmina
Program Coordinator, Odhikar

Thomas F. Farr
Director of Religious Freedom Project, Berkley Center for Religion, Peace, and World Affairs
First Director of U.S. State Department's Office of International Religious Freedom

Timothy Fort
Lindner-Gambal Professor of Business Ethics, George Washington University

Muhammad Gohar
Chairman, Video Cairo SAT

James K. Glassman
Founding Executive Director, George W. Bush Institute
Former Under Secretary for Public Diplomacy and Public Affairs

Bipul Gonsalves
Bangladesh Catholic Students Movement

Marc Gopin
James H. Laue Professor of World Religions, Diplomacy and Conflict, George Mason University
Director, Center for World Religions, Diplomacy and Conflict Resolution

Brian J. Grim
Senior Researcher and Director of Cross-National Data, Pew Forum on Religion & Public Life

Md. Zulfeqar Haider
Coordinator, Foreign Language Training Center

Catherine A. Hallock
Cultural Affairs Officer, The American Center, U.S. Embassy, Bangladesh

John Hamre
President and CEO, Center for Strategic and International Studies

Michael Hankey
Assistant Cultural Affairs Officer, U.S. Embassy, Egypt

Shah Abdul Hannan
Former Secretary, Government of Bangladesh
Chairman, Center for Strategic & Peace Studies

Abdel-Rahman Hassan
Cairo-based Imam

Khaled M. Hemaya
Cairo-based Imam

Allen Hertzke
Presidential Professor of Political Science, University of Oklahoma
Former Visiting Scholar, Brookings Institution

Joey R. Hood
First Secretary, Press, Education and Cultural Affairs, U.S. Embassy, Qatar

Kamal Hosain
Barrister-at-Law

Faria Naz Hossain
Consultant, Leaders of Influence (LOI) Program, The Asia Foundation

Cornelis Hulsman
Former Director, Center for Intercultural Dialogue and Translation and Editor-in-Chief,
Arab-West Report

David Hunsicker
Conflict and National Resources Specialist, USAID

Syed Anwar Husain
Professor of History, University of Dhaka

Saad Edin Ibrahim
Chairman of the Board, Ibn Khaldun Center for Development Studies

Morris Jacobs
Senior Vice President, Federal Division, PRO-telligent

Cynthia Farrell Johnson
Public Diplomacy Consultant

Douglas Johnston
President and Founder, International Center for Religion and Diplomacy
Former Executive Vice-President and COO, Center for Strategic and International Studies

Heshaam Kanona
Regional English Language Office, Office of Cultural Affairs, U.S. Embassy, Egypt

Javed Hyder Kareem
Director, Language Proficiency Center

Mostafa Abdul Karim
Cairo-based Imam

Adilur Rahman Khan
Secretary, Odhikar

Mohammad Mohabbat Khan
Seniormost Professor, University of Dhaka, Department of Public Administration

Suhail Khan
Senior Fellow for Christian-Muslim Understanding, Institute for Global Engagement

Rokhsana Khondker
Executive Director, Khan Foundation

Pankaj Aloysious Kondo
St. Joseph Catholic Church, Srimangal, Moulvibazar

Leonard Korycki
Office Director for Citizen Exchanges, U.S. Department of State

Lauren Kosa
Egypt Desk Officer, U.S. Department of State

Peter Kovach
Former Director, Office of International Religious Freedom, U.S. Department of State

Daniel T. Kuehl
Professor of Information Operations, National Defense University

Robert Tice Lalka
Global Partnerships Liaison, Office of the Secretary of State, U.S. Department of State

Amy J. Lillis

Office of International Religious Freedom, Bureau of Democracy, Human Rights and Labor, U.S. Department of State

Aaron Lobel
Founder and President, America Abroad Media

Sayed Mohammad Lokman
Director, Yanbu Cars Trading

Maryann Cusimano Love
Associate Professor of International Relations, The Catholic University of America

Haynes R. Mahoney
Counselor for Public Affairs (Culture and Press), U.S. Embassy, Egypt

Mandour S. Mandour
Vice Chancellor's Office, Al Azhar University

Talukder Maniruzzaman
National Professor and former Professor of Political Science, University of Dhaka

John Marks
Founder and President, Search for Common Ground

Jennifer Marshall
Director of Domestic Policy Studies and DeVos Center for Religion and Civil Society, Heritage Foundation

John Matheny
OSD(P) Policy Chair, Strategic Leadership Department

Andrea McDaniel
Co-founder and Managing Director, As We Forgive Rwanda Initiative
Former Director, Office of Private Sector Outreach, U.S. Department of State

Alexander McLaren
Public Diplomacy Officer, Office of International Religious Freedom, U.S. Department of State

Joshua L. Miller
Social Science Analyst, Evaluation and Measurement Unit
Office of the Under Secretary for Public Diplomacy and Public Affairs, U.S. Department of State

Andrew Mitchell
First Secretary & Cultural Affairs Officer, U.S. Embassy, Egypt

Marci Moberg
Conflict Program Assistant, Office of Conflict Management and Mitigation at USAID

Alamgir Mohiuddin
Editor, The Daily Naya Diganta

Ivdad Ahmed Khan Mojlish
Project Manager, Bangladesh Youth Leadership Center

Joannella Morales
Foreign Affairs Officer, Bureau of Democracy, Human Rights and Labor, U.S. Department of State

Abdeldayem Nossair
Special Advisor to the Grand Imam, General Secretary of World Association of Al-Azhar Graduates, Al-Azhar University's Advisor for Development of IT and Languages

Nafisa Nour
Engineering Teacher, Bangladesh

Stephanie Obenschain
Special Assistant to the Director of Policy, Planning and Resources for Public Diplomacy and Public Affairs, U.S. Department of State

Pius Pohdeung
Friar, OMI Oblate Fathers Lakhipur Mission, Bangladesh

Iftikhar Arman Rashid
Political & Economic Adviser, High Commission of Canada, Bangladesh

Russell Rochte
Faculty, National Defense Intelligence College

Alanna Rosenberg
Political Officer, U.S. Embassy, Greece

Hannah Rosenthal
Special Envoy, Office to Monitor and Combat Anti-Semitism, Bureau of Democracy, Human Rights and Labor, U.S. Department of State

Rick Ruth
Director, Office of Policy and Evaluation, Bureau of Educational and Cultural Affairs, U.S. Department of State

Khan Md. Sabbir

Teacher Trainer, Language Proficiency Center

Saira R. Saeed
Manager, Media Programs, Office of the Middle East Partnership Initiative

Ahmed Adly Said
Cairo-based Imam

Michael Collins Sarker
Friar, St. Joseph the Worker Parish, Srimangal, Bangladesh

Teresita C. Schaffer
Director of South Asia Program, Center for Strategic and International Affairs
Former U.S. Ambassador to Sri Lanka
Former Deputy Assistant Secretary of State for South Asian Affairs

Chris Seiple
President, The Institute for Global Engagement

Harvey W. Sernovitz
Press & Information Officer, The American Center, U.S. Embassy, Bangladesh

Leon Shahabian
Vice President and Treasurer, Layalina Productions
Senior Editor, The Layalina Review

Peter Shea
Second Secretary, Office of Economic and Political Affairs, U.S. Embassy, Egypt

Monica Shie
Public Diplomacy Officer, Office of Press and Public Diplomacy, U.S. Department of State

Andrew Sholomar
Finance Secretary, Bangladesh Indigenous People's Forum

Advocate Tanbir ul Islam Siddiqui
President, ChangeMakers

Youssef Sidhom
Chief Editor, Watani International, *Egypt*

Vineeta Singh
Transparency International

Stephen R. Snow

Former Senior Policy Analyst, USCIRF

Anne Speckhard
Adjunct Associate Professor, Georgetown University

Dan Sreebny
Acting Deputy Coordinator for Plans & Operations, Center for Strategic Counterterrorism Communication, U.S. Department of State
Former Acting Director, Global Strategic Engagement Center, U.S. Department of State

Christine Tadros
RSD Team Leader, Africa & Middle East Refugee Assistance (AMERA), Egypt

Flora Bably Talang
Secretary, Kuboraj Inter-punjee Development Association

Valentine Talang
Friar, OMI, Bangladesh

Shereef Tawfik
Cairo-based Imam

Knox Thames
Director of Policy and Research, USCIRF

Richard W. Timm
Catholic Educator, Hotline Human Rights Bangladesh

Vassilios Tsirbas
European Evangelical Alliance, Greece

Kilmeny Beckering Vinckers
Deputy High Commissioner, Australian High Commission, Bangladesh

Karin von Hippel
Senior Advisor to the State Department Counterterrorism Coordinator, U.S. Department of State

Raiqah Walie-Khan
Head of Performance, Marketing & Communications, British Council, Bangladesh

Joseph Witters
Public Affairs Specialist, U.S. Department of State

Joseph Wood
Senior Resident Fellow, The German Marshall Fund

Angela C. Wu
Director, Becket Institute, The Becket Fund for Religious Liberty

Rabeya Yasmin
Program Head, Ultra Poor Program, BRAC Centre

Muhammad Yousri
Civic Unit Media Manager, Video Cairo SAT

Suzette Zaki
Staff, U.S. Embassy, Egypt

[1] *National Security Strategy of the United States of America*, 2010, p. 1, http://www.whitehouse.gov/sites/default/files/rss_viewer/national_security_strategy.pdf.

[2] See Peter L. Berger, ed., *The Desecularization of the World: Resurgent Religion and World Politics* (Washington, D.C.: Ethics and Public Policy Center, 1999). Eighty-four percent of people who participated in a Gallup International survey declared religion to be an important part of their lives. "Religiosity Highest in World's Poorest Nations," Gallup International survey, August 31, 2010, http://www.gallup.com/poll/142727/religiosity-highest-world-poorest-nations.aspx.

[3] See "Promoting Interfaith Dialogue and Cooperation," The White House, http://www.whitehouse.gov/administration/eop/ofbnp/policy/interfaith. See also "A New Era of Partnerships: Report of Recommendations to the President." President's Advisory Council on Faith-Based and Neighborhood Partnerships. March 2010.

[4] Joint Chiefs of Staff, "Joint Publication 1-05: Religious Affairs in Joint Operations," November 13, 2009. See also Chris Seiple, "Ready...or Not? Equipping the U.S. Military Chaplain for Inter-Religious Liaison," *Review of Faith and International Affairs*, Winter 2009, http://www.informaworld.com/smpp/content~db=all~content=a921617134~frm=titlelink.

[5] "Religion, Conflict & Peacebuilding: An Introductory Guide," U.S. Agency for International Development, June 8, 2010, http://www.usaid.gov/our_work/crosscutting_programs/conflict/publications/Religion_Conflict_and_Peacebuilding_Toolkit.pdf. One-day trainings cover "the role religion and religious actors can play in conflict-sensitive development; diagnostic tools and key considerations for programming in religious contexts; and the Establishment Clause and legal principles that need to be taken into account during program design and implementation." The Foreign Service Institute has also established a course on Religion and Foreign Policy.

[6] "Engaging Religious Communities Abroad: A New Imperative for U.S. Foreign Policy," Chicago Council on Global Affairs, February 23, 2010, p. 1, http://www.thechicagocouncil.org/UserFiles/File/Task%20Force%20Reports/2010%20Religion%20Task%20Force_Full%20Report.pdf.

[7] "U.S. Religious Knowledge Survey," The Pew Forum on Religion & Public Life, Pew Research Center, September 28, 2010, http://www.pewforum.org/Other-Beliefs-and-Practices/U-S-Religious-Knowledge-Survey.aspx.

[8] These are: Buddhist, Hindu, Jewish, Jain, Muslim, Native American, Sikh, Afro-Caribbean, Baha'i, Confucian, Pagan, Shinto, Taoist, and Zoroastrian. The Pluralism Project at Harvard University, http://pluralism.org/ocg/index/php. About 1,500 religions are recognized in the United States.

[9] Grim, "The Demographics of Faith."

[10] The 1663 Rhode Island Charter recognized that "a most flourishing civill state may stand and best bee maintained...with a full libertie in religious concernements; and that true pietye rightly grounded upon gospel principles, will give the best and greatest security to sovereignetye." "Charter of Rhode Island and Providence Plantations—July 15, 1663," The Avalon Project, Yale Law School, http://avalon.law.yale.edu/17th_century/ri04.asp. See also the 1786 Virginia Statute of Religion. "Act for Establishing Religious Freedom, January 16, 1786," Virginia Memory, Library of Virginia, http://www.virginiamemory.com/online_classroom/shaping_the_constitution/doc/religious_freedom. See "Historical Context," Virginia Wesleyan College, http://www.vwc.edu/academics/csrf/issues/historicalcontext.php for a brief overview of religious freedom in colonial times.

[11] Barack H. Obama, "On a New Beginning," speech, Cairo University, June 4, 2009.

[12] "Obama remarks during Iftar dinner at the White House," speech transcript, August 13, 2010, http://projects.washingtonpost.com/obama-speeches/speech/364/.

[13] Franklin D. Roosevelt, State of the Union Address to the Congress, January 6, 1941.

[14] UN General Assembly. *Universal Declaration of Human Rights*, December 10, 1948, 217 A (III), http://www.unhcr.org/refworld/docid/3ae6b3712c.html.

[15] U.S. Congress. *International Religious Freedom Act of 1998*, H.R 2431, 105th Congress, second session, http://www.state.gov/documents/organization/2297.pdf.

[16] Obama, "On a New Beginning."

[17] Brian J. Grim and Roger Finke, "Religious Persecution in Cross-National Context: Clashing Civilizations or Regulated Religious Economies?" *American Sociological Review*, August 2007, http://asr.sagepub.com/content/72/4/633.full.pdf+html. See also Grim and Finke, *Price of Freedom Denied: Religious Persecution and Conflict in the 21st Century* (New York: Cambridge University Press, 2011).

[18] Percentages by region were 93 percent in Latin America, 84 percent in Eastern Europe, 92 percent in the Middle East, 93 percent in Asia and 98 percent in Africa. "Global Unease with Major World Powers," The Pew Global Attitudes Project, Pew Research Center, June 27, 2007, http://pewglobal.org/2007/06/27/global-unease-with-major-world-powers/.

[19] Concept from Chris Seiple (president of the Institute for Global Engagement), interview with the author, Washington, D.C., November 2009.

[20] Commissioner Elizabeth Prodromou describes how the International Religious Freedom Act institutionalized U.S. commitment to safeguarding religious freedom and not merely responding to religious persecution, and she warns against any "false dichotomies pitting human rights against peacebuilding, quiet diplomacy over activist public advocacy, and incentives against penalties." She also argues that "by sending an unambiguous signal to CPCs that egregious violations of religious freedom are intolerable, Washington will strengthen its soft power." Prodromou, "Election 2008: Day-After Policies for International Religious Freedom," *Review of Faith and International Affairs*, Fall 2008, p. 17.

[21] Barack H. Obama, "Remarks by the President at the Acceptance of the Nobel Peace Prize," speech, Oslo City Hall, December 10, 2009.

[22] Robert A. Seiple, "Methodology, Metrics, and Moral Imperatives in Religious Freedom Diplomacy," *Review of Faith and International Affairs*, Summer 2008, p. 53. Also, former Secretary of State Madeleine Albright writes about promotion of religious liberty: "Lasting change is more likely to come through persuasion than by making blunt demands." Albright, *The Mighty and the Almighty: Reflections on America, God, and World Affairs* (New York: Harper Perennial, 2006), p. 97.

[23] Thomas F. Farr, *World of Faith and Freedom: Why International Religious Freedom is Vital to American National Security* (New York: Oxford University Press, 2008), p. 185.

[24] Kristin Lord and Marc Lynch write: "Public engagement is also used most effectively in concert with other instruments of power, as a sort of diplomatic force-multiplier that can amplify the impact of agile diplomacy, effective development activities and successful military operations." Lord and Lynch, "America's Extended Hand: Assessing the Obama Administration's Global Engagement Strategy," Center for a New American Security, May 19, 2010, p. 4, http://www.cnas.org/node/4485.

[25] The USCIRF 2010 Annual Report argues that "religious freedom provides the foundation for any successful interreligious dialogue or engagement of religious actors." U.S. Commission on International Religious Freedom, *Annual Report 2010*, May 2010, p. 18, http://www.uscirf.gov/images/annual%20report%202010.pdf.

[26] As Lord and Lynch note: "The Department's most senior military and civilian leaders, most prominently Secretary Gates and Admiral Mullen, the chairman of the Joint Chiefs of Staff, have advocated a greater sensitivity to public opinion overseas and the messages conveyed by American actions, not just words…a move away from one-way strategies focused on 'messaging' in favor of strategies focused more on dialogue." "America's Extended Hand," p. 68.

[27] Recent reports have called for the integration of public diplomacy and religious freedom, including Thomas F. Farr and Dennis R. Hoover, "The Future of U.S. International Religious Freedom Policy: Recommendations for the Obama Administration," Georgetown University and the Institute for Global Engagement, March 18, 2009, http://www.globalengage.org/research/reports/829-the-future-of-us-international-religious-freedom-policy-special-report-.html and "Engaging Religious Communities Abroad." On page 31 of the "The Future of U.S. International Religious Freedom Policy," Farr writes: "U.S. public diplomacy must develop the capacity to convey accurately the importance of religion in American history and in contemporary American society, our own struggles with religious freedom, the role of religion in other societies that have become (or are in the process of becoming) liberal democracies, and our intent to assist other countries working to secure stable, healthy religion-state relations."

[28] Diplomacy, communications, development assistance and domestic involvement are all central features of a more holistic approach to global engagement on religious freedom. The components of global engagement are described at "Statement by the President on the White House Organization for Homeland Security and Counterterrorism," The White House, May 26, 2009,

http://www.whitehouse.gov/the_press_office/Statement-by-the-President-on-the-White-House-Organization-for-Homeland-Security-and-Counterterrorism/

[29] Judith McHale, "Public Diplomacy: Strengthening U.S. Engagement with the World," February 26, 2010, http://www.uscpublicdiplomacy.org/pdfs/PD_US_World_Engagement.pdf.

[30] Ibid., p. 8.

[31] See, for example, Robert Reilly, "Ideas Matter: Restoring the Content of Public Diplomacy," The Heritage Foundation, July 27, 2009, http://www.heritage.org/research/reports/2009/07/ideas-matter-restoring-the-content-of-public-diplomacy.

[32] Chereeka Montgomery, comments at the U.S. Advisory Commission on Public Diplomacy July 2010 Official Meeting, Washington, DC, July 20, 2010.

[33] "2010 Arab Public Opinion Poll," University of Maryland with Zogby International, Brookings Institution, http://www.brookings.edu/reports/2010/0805_arab_opinion_poll_telhami.aspx.

[34] McHale, "Public Diplomacy," p. 8.

[35] Douglas Johnston, president and founder of the International Center for Religion and Diplomacy and former deputy assistant secretary of the Navy, has promoted a concept of faith-based diplomacy that draws on the principles and practices of religion. See Johnston, *Faith-Based Diplomacy: Trumping Realpolitik* (New York: Oxford University Press, 2003). Chris Seiple, president of The Institute for Global Engagement and a former Captain serving in the Commandant of the Marine Corps' think tank, has run several programs abroad based on his idea of relational diplomacy: simultaneous and transparent engagement—both top-down and bottom-up—to yield roadmap agreement about how to build religious freedom at the intersection of culture and the rule of law. See "The Center for Relational Diplomacy," Institute for Global Engagement, http://www.globalengage.org/diplomacy/about.html. Read more about their programs beginning on p. 64.

[36] McHale, "Public Diplomacy," p. 8.

[37] See discussion in "Engaging Religious Communities Abroad," p. 39-42.

[38] Peter Kovach (then director of the Office of International Religious Freedom at U.S. Department of State), interview with the author, Washington, D.C., April 2010.

[39] For example, David Arulanantham (political officer), interview with the author, Dhaka, April 2010.

[40] These principles may be relevant to all diplomats, given that "in the new paradigm of public diplomacy, diplomats more consciously represent their whole society to the host society, beyond traditional government-to-government communication." Jeremy Kinsman, "A Diplomat's Handbook for Democracy Development Support," Community of Democracies, 2010, p. 28, http://www.diplomatshandbook.org/pdf/Diplomats_Handbook.pdf.

[41] These categories are not intended to represent a comprehensive communications engagement strategy, but the steps are loosely based on a basic information campaign model, the elements of which include: the desired effect, audience, message, delivery method and evaluation. See, for example, Daniel T. Kuehl, "Information Management, Strategic Communication, Strategic Influence: Their Relationship in the Information Environment," Information Resources Management College, National Defense University. Theories in the field of communications are constantly developing. A comprehensive public-diplomacy campaign will account for an understanding of communication not only as the repeated, one-way transmission of a message, but as a complex "meaning-making process" that requires communicators to deemphasize control, use experimental variation and consider moves to disrupt the existing system. See Steven R. Corman, Angela Trethewey, and Bud Goodall, "A 21st Century Model for Communication in the Global War of Ideas," Consortium for Strategic Communication, Arizona State University, April 3, 2007, http://comops.org/article/114.pdf.

[42] "Global Restrictions on Religion," Pew Forum on Religion & Public Life, Pew Research Center, December 17, 2009, http://pewforum.org/Government/Global-Restrictions-on-Religion.aspx.

[43] U.S. Department of State, Bureau of Democracy, Human Rights, and Labor, International Religious Freedom Office, *Preface: International Religious Freedom Report 2009*, October 26, 2009, http://www.america.gov/st/texttrans-english/2009/October/20091027112026eaifas0.8861811.html.

[44] *Universal Declaration of Human Rights*, Article 18. Farr further defines religious freedom as "the right to pursue the religious quest, to embrace or reject the interior and public obligations that ensue, and to enter or exit religious communities that reflect, or do not reflect, one's understanding of religious truth." Farr, *World of Faith and Freedom*, p. 22.

[45] *International Religious Freedom Act*, Sec. 2.

[46] "Global Restrictions on Religion," p. 8.

[47] U.S. Department of State, Bureau of Democracy, Human Rights, and Labor, International Religious Freedom Office, *Executive Summary: International Religious Freedom Report 2010*, November 17, 2010, http://www.state.gov/g/drl/rls/irf/2010/148659.htm. USCIRF has also offered a framework to categorize government restrictions on religious freedom, describing three types of government restrictions: 1) State-sponsored hostility and repression of religion, including active steps to prohibit religious freedom of individuals or communities; 2) State-sponsored extremist ideology and education, including sponsorship of education systems that teach hatred of certain religious groups; and 3) State failure to prevent and punish religious freedom violations (impunity), including failure to respond to violence against certain religious individuals or communities. Commissioners'remarks, Release of the United States Commission on International Religious Freedom *Annual Report 2010*, Washington, D.C., April 29, 2010.

[48] H. Knox Thames, Chris Seiple, and Amy Rowe, *International Religious Freedom Advocacy: A Guide to Organizations, Law, and NGOs* (Waco, TX: Baylor University Press, 2009), p. 11-14.

[49] "Global Restrictions on Religion," p. 17.

[50] "Two Years of Sectarian Violence: What Happened? Where Do We Begin?" Egyptian Initiative for Personal Rights, April 2006, p. 5, http://www.eipr.org/en/report/2010/04/11/776/778. Egypt, which has been on USCIRF's Watch List since 2002, "has not taken sufficient steps to halt the repression of and discrimination against Christians and other religious believers, or, in many cases, to punish those responsible for violence or other severe violations of religious freedom. This increase in violence, and the failure to prosecute those responsible, fosters a growing climate of impunity." USCIRF, Annual Report 2010, p. 227.

[51] Angela Wu (Director, Becket Institute, The Becket Fund for Religious Liberty), interview with the author, Washington, D.C., December 2009.

[52] "Global Restrictions on Religion," p. 30.

[53] *International Religious Freedom Act of 1998*.

[54] The current CPCs include Burma, China, Eritrea, Iran, North Korea, Saudi Arabia, Sudan and Uzbekistan. See "Countries of Particular Concern," U.S. Department of State, http://www.state.gov/g/drl/irf/c13281.htm.

[55] *International Religious Freedom Act*, Title IV.

[56] "Secretary of State Rice in September 2005 announced the denial of commercial export to Eritrea of defense articles and services covered by the Arms Control Export Act..." U.S. Commission on International Religious Freedom, *Annual Report 2006*, May 2006, p. 84, http://www.uscirf.gov/reports-and-briefs/annual-report/3342-2006-annual-report.html.

[57] U.S. Department of State, Bureau of Democracy, Human Rights, and Labor, International Religious Freedom Office, *Country Reports: 2010 Report on International Religious Freedom*, 2010, http://www.state.gov/g/drl/irf/rpt/.

[58] In 2011, USCIRF recommended that the secretary of state designate the following 14 countries as CPCs: Burma, China, Eritrea, Iran, North Korea, Saudi Arabia, Sudan, Uzbekistan, Egypt, Iraq, Nigeria, Pakistan, Turkmenistan, and Vietnam. See "Countries of Particular Concern," U.S. Commission on International Religious Freedom, http://www.uscirf.gov/countries/countries-of-particular-concern.html.

[59] USCIRF has placed the following 11 countries on the Watch List for 2011: Afghanistan, Belarus, Cuba, India, Indonesia, Laos, Russia, Somalia, Tajikistan, Turkey and Venezuela. See "Watch List Countries," U.S. Commission on International Religious Freedom, http://www.uscirf.gov/countries/watch-list-countries.html.

[60] Leonard A. Leo, "Message from the Chair," USCIRF, http://www.uscirf.gov/about-uscirf/message-from-the-chair.html.

[61] See the "Frequently Asked Questions," USCIRF, http://www.uscirf.gov/about-uscirf/frequently-asked-questions.html.

[62] For example, the Afghan convert to Christianity Sayed Mussa, who faces the prospect of a death sentence for apostasy, said that he had received better treatment since the U.S. Embassy intervened. Ray Rivera, "Afghan Rights Fall Short For Christian Converts," *New York Times*, February 6, 2011, p. 8.

[63] Thomas F. Farr and William L. Saunders, Jr., "The Bush Administration and America's International Religious Freedom Policy," *Harvard Journal of Law and Public Policy*, June 2009, p. 950-951, 958, http://www.harvard-jlpp.com/wp-content/uploads/2009/05/FarrFinal.pdf.

[64] For a list of USCIRF's recent accomplishments, see the USCIRF 2011 Annual Report. U.S. Commission on International Religious Freedom, *Annual Report 2011*, May 2011, p. 5-6, http://www.uscirf.gov/reports-and-briefs/annual-report/3594-2011-annual-report.html

[65] Farr, *World of Faith and Freedom*, p. 114.

[66] Ibid., p. 41, 137.

[67] Carol Lee Hamrin, "A New Framework for Promoting Religious Freedom in China," *Review of Faith & International Affairs*, Spring 2005, p. 4.

[68] Farr and Saunders, "The Bush Administration and America's International Religious Freedom Policy," p. 964, 965.

[69] Joannella Morales (Foreign Affairs Officer, Office of International Religious Freedom, U.S. Department of State), interview with the author, Washington D.C., July 2010.

[70] For a full description of these efforts, see programs section, p. 43.

[71] James Glassman, "Public Diplomacy for the 21st Century," speech, Council on Foreign Relations, June 30, 2008, http://www.america.gov/st/texttrans-english/2008/July/20080702123054xjsnommis0.3188745.html.

[72] José Casanova, "Balancing Religious Freedom and Cultural Preservation," Review of Faith and International Affairs, Summer 2008, p. 13-16.

[73] Rick Ruth (Director, Office of Policy and Evaluation, Bureau of Educational and Cultural Affairs, U.S. Department of State), interview with the author, Washington D.C., October 2009.

[74] "Evaluation of the Youth Exchange & Study Program: Final Report," Final Report prepared by Intermedia for U.S. Department of State Bureau of Educational and Cultural Affairs, August 2009, p. 33, http://exchanges.state.gov/media/pdfs/youth/yes_final_evaluation_report_august_2009.pdf.

[75] Ibid., p. 20, 22.

[76] Ibid., p. 48.

[77] Yousef Sidhom (Chief Editor, *Watani International*), interview with the author, Cairo, August 2010.

[78] Aaron Lobel (*Founder and President, America Abroad Media*), interview with the author, Washington, D.C., December 2009.

[79] Interviews with the author, Dhaka, April 2010. The Commission placed Bangladesh on its Watch List from 2005 to 2008, in part because of violence against religious minorities. With improvements after the 2008 elections, Bangladesh was removed from the list in 2009. However, that year's report maintained that "although the constitution provides protections for women and minorities, Hindus, Buddhists, Christians, Ahmadis, and other minorities must regularly grapple with societal discrimination, as well as face prejudice that hinders their ability to access public services, the legal system, and government, military, and police employment." U.S. Commission on International Religious Freedom, *2009 Annual Report*, May 2009, p. 218-219, http://www.uscirf.gov/images/final%20ar2009%20with%20cover.pdf.

[80] U.S. Department of State, Bureau of Democracy, Human Rights, and Labor, International Religious Freedom Office, *Introduction: International Religious Freedom Report 2009*, October 26, 2009, http://www.state.gov/g/drl/rls/irf/2009/127214.htm.

[81] *Universal Declaration of Human Rights*, Article 18; Council of Europe. *The European Convention on Human Rights and Its Five Protocols*, November 4, 1950, Article 9, http://www.hri.org/docs/ECHR50.html; UN General Assembly. *International Covenant on Civil and Political Rights*, March 23, 1976, 2200 A (XXI), Article 18, http://www2.ohchr.org/english/law/ccpr.htm; UN General Assembly. *Declaration on the Elimination of all Forms of Intolerance and Discrimination Based on Religion or Belief*, November 25, 1981, 36/55, http://www2.ohchr.org/english/law/religion.htm.

[82] *International Covenant on Civil and Political Rights*, Preamble.

[83] Kevin Seamus Hasson, *The Right to Be Wrong* (San Francisco: Encounter Books, 2005), p. 118.

[84] Constitutional law expert Michael J. Perry describes the rationale this way: "We detest and oppose states of affairs in which human beings—*any human beings, not just those for whom we have special affection, such as family, friends, countrymen*—suffer grievously in consequence of laws and other policies that are misguided or worse. We detest and oppose such states of affairs, because we detest and oppose such suffering. And so we work to build a world in which such suffering is, over time, diminished." Michael J. Perry, "Secular Worldviews, Religious Worldviews, And The Morality Of Human Rights," in Charles Taliaferro, Steven Goetz, and Victoria S. Harrison, eds., *The Routledge Companion to Theism*, forthcoming, p. 16.

81

[85] Farr and Saunders, "The Bush Administration and America's International Religious Freedom Policy," p. 951-952.

[86] Grim and Finke, *Price of Freedom Denied*, p. 18-19.

[87] In Egypt, for example, a local human rights organization cites 53 incidents of sectarian violence or tension from January 2008 to January 2010, spread out over more than half of Egypt's governorates. Those incidents included acts of collective retribution, violence against people conducting religious rites and premeditated murder on the basis of religious identity. "Two Years of Sectarian Violence," p. 6-9.

[88] Grim and Finke, *Price of Freedom Denied*, p. 19.

[89] Ibid., p. 23, 71.

[90] John Witte, Jr., and Johan D. van der Vyver, eds., *Religious Human Rights In Global Perspective: Religious Perspectives* (Cambridge, MA: Martinus Nijhoff Publishers, 1996).

[91] Grim and Finke, *Price of Freedom Denied*, p. 205.

[92] Grim and Finke, "Religious Persecution in Cross-National Context," p.654; and Grim and Finke, *Price of Freedom Denied*, p. 78.

[93] Brian J. Grim, "God's Economy: Religious Freedom & Socio-Economic Wellbeing," in Paul Marshall, ed., *Religious Freedom in the World* (Lanham, MD: Rowman and Littlefield, 2008).

[94] Harris Mylonas in "Report of the Georgetown Symposium on Religion, Democracy and the Foreign Policy of the Obama Administration," Berkley Center for Religion, Peace, and World Affairs, June 7, 2010, p 17, http://repository.berkleycenter.georgetown.edu/20090903_Democracy.pdf.

[95] Philip Jenkins, "The Politics of Persecuted Religious Minorities," in Robert Seiple and Dennis Hoover, eds., *Religion and Security: The New Nexus in International Relations* (Lanham, MD: Rowman and Littlefield, 2004), p. 26.

[96] Ragnhild Nordås, "State Religiosity and Civil War: Does Religious Heterogeneity and the Role of Religion in States Influence the Risk of Intrastate Armed Conflict?" Centre for the Study of Civil War, 2004.

[97] Toft, God's Century, p. 220.

[98] Shadi Hamid, "The Islamist Response to Repression: Are Mainstream Islamist Groups Radicalizing?" The Brookings Institution, August 9, 2010, http://www.brookings.edu/papers/2010/0809_islamist_groups_hamid.aspx.

[99] Chris Seiple and Joshua White, "Uzbekistan and the Central Asian Crucible of Religion and Security," in Seiple and Hoover, *Religion and Security*.

[100] Toft, God's Century, p. 142.

[101] He also notes interesting implications for policies on racial or religious profiling. Brett Scharffs, "Security, Religious Autonomy, and the Good Society," *Review of Faith and International Affairs*, Fall 2007, p. 8.

[102] Grim and Finke, *Price of Freedom Denied*, p. 101-104.

[103] Alejandro J. Beutel, "Data on Post-9/11 Terrorism in the United States," Policy Report, Muslim Public Affairs Council, January 2011.

[104] Joint Chiefs of Staff, "Joint Publication 1-05: Religious Affairs in Joint Operations."

[105] Ibid., Appendix A.

[106] Farr, *World of Faith and Freedom*, p. 19.

[107] Grim, "God's Economy."

[108] Ibid.

[109] Economic freedom is measured by the Heritage Foundation/Wall Street Journal Indices of Economic Freedom. Theodore Malloch, "Free to Choose: Economics and Religion" in Marshall, ed., *Religious Freedom in the World*.

[110] Ibid.

[111] Brian J. Grim (Senior Researcher and Director of Cross-National Data), interview with the author, Washington D.C., October 2009.

[112] Malloch, "Free to Choose."

[113] Rodney Stark and William Bainbridge, *A Theory of Religion* (New York: David Lang, 1987), p.108.

[114] Charles M. North and Carl R. Gwin, "Religious Freedom and Unintended Consequences of State Religion," *Southern Economic Journal*, July 2004.

[115] For a discussion of the reasons why religion may be good for economic development, see Rachel M. McCleary, "The Economics of Religion and Secularization," *Review of Faith and International Affairs*, Spring 2007, p. 44.

[116] See Hamrin, "A New Framework for Promoting Religious Freedom in China," p. 4.

[117] Bruce Sacerdote and Edward L. Glaeser, "Education and Religion," National Bureau of Economic Research Working Paper, January 2001, http://www.nber.org/papers/w8080.pdf.

[118] Robert J. Barro and Rachel M. McCleary, "Religion and Economic Growth," *American Sociological Review*, October 2003.

[119] Hamrin, "A New Framework for Promoting Religious Freedom in China."

[120] Brian J. Grim in "Report of the Georgetown Symposium on Religion, Democracy and the Foreign Policy of the Obama Administration," p.12.

[121] See Paul Marshall, "The Range of Religious Freedom," in Marshall, ed., *Religious Freedom in the World*.

[122] See, for example, Farr, *World of Faith and Freedom*, p. 271.

[123] "Engaging Religious Communities Abroad," p. 45.

[124] W. Cole Durham, Jr., "Legal Status of Religious Organizations: A Comparative Overview," *Review of Faith and International Affairs*, Summer 2010, p. 9.

[125] Daniel Philpott, "Explaining the Political Ambivalence of Religion," *American Political Science Review*, August 2007, p. 506-507.

[126] Monica Duffy Toft, Daniel Philpott, and Timothy Samuel Shah, *God's Century: Resurgent Religion and Global Politics* (New York: W.W. Norton & Company, 2011), p. 120.

[127] Daniel Philpott, "New Trends in the Data on Religion and Democracy," in "Report of the Georgetown Symposium on Religion, Democracy and the Foreign Policy of the Obama Administration," p. 11-14.

[128] Prodromou, "Election 2008," p. 18. In Asia and Africa, the Indian jurist Tahir Mahmood notes three models of religion-state relations: one in which a particular religious faith is either recognized as the state religion or otherwise given a prime position by the constitution and the basic laws; one in which there is no official religion and the state has no constitutionally assigned or legally sanctioned role to play in religious affairs; and one in which there is no officially adopted state religion but the state can have a legally permissible role in the affairs of religion. In the first model, he notes that "most of the countries with a constitutionally proclaimed official or otherwise privileged religion do, at the same time, guarantee to all their citizens freedom of religion—belief and practice—and also formally assure their religious minorities of their legitimate rights as per international norms." Tahir Mahmood, "Legal Regulation of Religion in the Third World: Afro-Asian Paradigms," *Review of Faith and International Affairs*, Summer 2010, p. 37.

[129] Over the years, the constitutional delineation of appropriate interaction between state and religion has become increasingly clear. The Orthodox Church has also moved toward less dependence on the state. See Alfred Stepan, "Religion, Democracy, and the 'Twin Tolerations,'" in Larry Diamond, Mark F. Plattner, and Philip J. Costopoulos, eds., *World Religions and Democracy* (Baltimore: The Johns Hopkins University Press, 2005), p. 20.

[130] Emile Nakhleh, "Engagement for the Common Good," The Immanent Frame, May 25, 2010, http://blogs.ssrc.org/tif/2010/05/25/engagement-for-the-common-good/. It is worth noting that while some countries with Islam as the national religion do not provide protections for free assembly and speech that match international standards, others do provide for these freedoms. Tad Stahnke and Robert C. Britt, "The Religion-State Relationship and the Right to Freedom of Religion or Belief: A Comparative Textual Analysis of the Constitutions of Predominantly Muslim Countries," USCIRF, March 2005, http://www.uscirf.gov/images/stories/pdf/Comparative_Constitutions/Study0305.pdf.

[131] Farr, *World of Faith and Freedom*, p. 7. See also "Religious Freedom in Afghanistan: Challenges for U.S. Foreign Policy," Berkley Center for Religion, Peace, and World Affairs, June 2009, http://berkleycenter.georgetown.edu/resources/topics/religion-and-conflict-case-studies/subtopics/afghanistan-religious-freedom-and-us-foreign-policy.

[132] Knox Thames, "Strategic Engagement of Religious Actors in Afghanistan," Berkley Center for Religion, Peace, and World Affairs, October 28, 2010.

[133] "Engaging Religious Communities Abroad," p. 11.

[134] Ibid.

[135] For example, former Secretary of the Government of Bangladesh Shah Abdul Hannan argues that because the secular movement separated education and religion, "man became more accustomed to

immorality and selfishness." Shah Abdul Hannan (Former Secretary, Government of Bangladesh), "Education, Religion & Secularism."

[136] See José Casanova, *Public Religions in the Modern World* (Chicago: The University of Chicago Press, 1994), p. 223. See also Philpott in "Report of the Georgetown Symposium on Religion, Democracy and the Foreign Policy of the Obama Administration," p. 11-14.

[137] Chris Seiple writes, "liberty was defined not as the opposite of religious fundamentalism, namely secular fundamentalism, but rather as *religious pluralism*." Chris Seiple, "Memo to the State: Religion and Security," *Review of Faith and International Affairs*, Spring 2007, p. 40.

[138] Farr and Hoover, "The Future of U.S. International Religious Freedom Policy," p. 32-33.

[139] Jeffrey Stout, *Democracy and Tradition* (Princeton: Princeton University Press, 2004), p. 63. As President Obama has said, "Secularists are wrong when they ask believers to leave their religion at the door before entering into the public square. Frederick Douglas, Abraham Lincoln, Williams Jennings Bryan, Dorothy Day, Martin Luther King—indeed, the majority of great reformers in American history—were not only motivated by faith, but repeatedly used religious language to argue for their cause. So to say that men and women should not inject their 'personal morality' into public policy debates is a practical absurdity. Our law is by definition a codification of morality, much of it grounded in the Judeo-Christian tradition." Obama, speech, "Call to Renewal Keynote Address," Washington, D.C., June 28, 2006.

[140] Lemon v. Kurtzman, 403 U.S. 602 (1971). Interestingly, a recent poll showed that many Americans believe constitutional restrictions on religion in public schools are stricter than they really are. "U.S. Religious Knowledge Survey."

[141] Organizations receiving USAID funds may retain their religious character and may offer religious activities as long as they are held separately from the government-funded activities and on a voluntary basis. Stanley Carlson-Thies, "The U.S. Government and Faith-based Organizations: Keeping the Uneasy Alliance on Firm Ground," *Review of Faith and International Affairs*, Summer 2010.

[142] For further discussion see Michael Kessler, "Establishment Clause Doesn't Limit Foreign Policy," *On Faith, Washington Post*, February 26, 2010, http://onfaith.washingtonpost.com/onfaith/georgetown/2010/02/why_the_establishment_clause_doesnt_lim it_presidential_foreign_policy.html
Also, in Hein v. Freedom From Religion Foundation, 551 U.S. 587 (2007), the Supreme Court found that taxpayers cannot challenge the constitutionality of executive branch activities on the basis that it violates the Establishment Clause.

[143] Lamont v. Woods, 948 F.2d 825, 832 (2nd Cir. 1991).

[144] Jessica Powley Hayden, "Mullahs on a Bus: The Establishment Clause and U.S. Foreign Aid," *The Georgetown Law Journal*, 2006, http://www.georgetownlawjournal.org/issues/pdf/95-1/hayden.pdf%5B1%5D.pdf.

[145] Frederick D. Barton, Shannon Hayden, and Karin von Hippel, "Navigating in the Fog: Improving U.S. Government Engagement with Religion," in *Rethinking Religion and World Affairs*, Monica Duffy Toft, Timothy S. Shah and Alfred C. Stepan, eds., Oxford University Press, forthcoming 2011.

[146] U.S. Agency for International Development, Office of Inspector General, "Audit of USAID's Faith-Based and Community Initiatives," July 17, 2009, p. 26, http://www.usaid.gov/oig/public/fy09rpts/9-000-09-009-p.pdf.

[147] "Religion, Conflict & Peacebuilding," p. 7.

[148] "Audit of USAID's Faith-Based and Community Initiatives," p. 23.

[149] Ibid., p.1.

[150] "Engaging Religious Communities Abroad," p. 64.

[151] See Barton, "Navigating in the Fog," as well as the Chicago Council Report, which has called for "the president of the United States, advised by executive branch offices and agencies who have studied the problem, to clarify that the Establishment Clause does not bar the United States from engaging religious communities abroad in the conduct of foreign policy, though it does impose constraints on the means that the United States may choose to pursue this engagement." "Engaging Religious Communities Abroad," p. 65.

[152] John Hanford in Rosalind I. J. Hackett, Mark Silk, and Dennis Hoover, eds., "Religious Persecution as a U.S. Policy Issue: Proceedings of a Consultation held at Trinity College," Center for the Study of Religion in Public Life, September 26-27, 1999, p.55, http://www.trincoll.edu/depts/csrpl/Religious%20Persecution/relperse.pdf.

[153] Jeremy Gunn in "Religious Persecution as a U.S. Policy Issue," p. 48-50. See also Farr, *World of Faith and Freedom*, p. 126. Farr also explains how officials have determined whether persecution was religiously based by using a "significance standard" in which "if religion was a significant element in explaining religious persecution, we called it religious persecution." Farr, *World of Faith and Freedom*, p. 174.

[154] The United States has "a long bipartisan track record of unilateral U.S. efforts supporting international human rights, including religious freedom." Farr and Hoover, "The Future of U.S. International Religious Freedom Policy," p. 46.

[155] *National Security Strategy of the United States*, p. 35.

[156] Ibid.

[157] "Frequently Asked Questions," USCIRF, http://www.uscirf.gov/about-uscirf/frequently-asked-questions.html. See also John Witte, Jr., "Soul Wars: New Battles, New Norms," *Review of Faith and International Affairs*, Spring 2007, p. 14.

[158] "Global Unease with Major World Powers," The Pew Global Attitudes Project.

[159] Andrew Albertson, Barak Hoffman, and Tuqa Nusairat, eds., "After Cairo: From the Vision of the Cairo Speech to Active Support for Human Dignity," Project on Middle East Democracy, January 2010, p. 8, http://pomed.org/wordpress/wp-content/uploads/2010/01/after_cairo_january_2010.pdf. Also, Gallup World Poll data has suggested that the majority of Muslims around the world do not want religious leaders to directly lead their countries. For example, 74 percent of Turks, 56 percent of Iranians, and 53 percent of Indonesians would reject clerics being directly involved in writing national legislation. Rheault, Magali and Dalia Mogahed, "Majorities See Religion and Democracy as Compatible," Gallup News Service, October 3, 2007, http://www.gallup.com/poll/28762/Majorities-Muslims-Americans-See-Religion-Law-Compatible.aspx.

[160] Casanova, "Balancing Religious Freedom and Cultural Preservation."

[161] Winnifred F. Sullivan in "Religious Persecution as a U.S. Policy Issue," p. 48. For a full discussion from Sullivan, see for example *The Impossibility of Religious Freedom* (Princeton: Princeton University Press, 2005). Sullivan argues that religion cannot be coherently defined for the purposes of American law.

[162] Stephen McDougal, review of *Freedom of Religion: UN and European Human Rights Law and Practice* by Paul M. Taylor (New York: Cambridge University Press, 2005), http://www.bsos.umd.edu/gvpt/lpbr/subpages/reviews/taylor0806.htm. Based on a perception that the UDHR came from a secular, Judeo-Christian context, the Organization of the Islamic Conference adopted the Cairo Declaration on Human Rights in Islam in 1990, emphasizing that it is prohibited to "exercise any form of compulsion on man or to exploit his poverty or ignorance in order to convert him to another religion or to atheism." Organization of the Islamic Conference, *Cairo Declaration on Human Rights in Islam*, August 5, 1990, Article 10.

[163] Witte, "Soul Wars," p. 14.

[164] Witte, *God's Joust, God's Justice*, p. 109. The interfaith activist Eboo Patel concurs: "Today, people spend less time encapsulated by the institutions of their traditional communities and more time in spaces where there are frequent interactions between people of diverse backgrounds." Eboo Patel, "Affirming Identity, Achieving Pluralism: Insights from Interfaith Youth Work," *Review of Faith and International Affairs*, Spring 2007, p. 22.

[165] Farr and Hoover, "The Future of U.S. International Religious Freedom Policy," p. 16.

[166] Hoover, "In Defense of Organized Religion."

[167] Casanova, "Balancing Religious Freedom and Cultural Preservation," p. 13-16. See also Casanova, "Religious Freedom: For and Against Proselytism," The Immanent Frame, April 26, 2010, http://blogs.ssrc.org/tif/2010/04/26/proselytism/. Pluralism can be defined as not only diversity and tolerance, but the active engagement and understanding that comes from an encounter of commitments based on dialogue. See Diana L. Eck's definition of pluralism at the Pluralism Project: "What is Pluralism?" The Pluralism Project at Harvard University, http://pluralism.org/pages/pluralism/what_is_pluralism.

[168] See, for example, "The Dangerous Idea of Protecting Religions from 'Defamation': A Threat to Universal Human Rights Standards," Policy Focus, United States Commission on International Religious Freedom, November 11, 2009. See also "Defamation of Religions," Becket Fund for Religious Liberty Issues Brief, June 2008.

[169] "The Dangerous Idea of Protecting Religions from 'Defamation,'" p. 1.

[170] Jane Morse, "Freedom of Speech and Religion Must Be Balanced, Clinton Says," America.gov, October 26, 2009, http://www.america.gov/st/democracyhr-english/2009/October/20091026163650ajesroM0.8743555.html.

[171] USCIRF, *Annual Report 2010*. In 2011, the UN Human Rights Council adopted a resolution against religious intolerance, rather than one "combating defamation of religions." USCIRF, *Annual Report 2011*, p. 6.

[172] As Clinton said at the same briefing, "The United States will always seek to counter negative stereotypes of individuals based on their religion and will stand against discrimination and persecution." Morse, "Freedom of Speech and Religion Must Be Balanced, Clinton Says."

[173] See Abram Shulsky and Douglas J. Feith, "Organizing the U.S. Government to Counter Hostile Ideologies," Hudson Institute Briefing Paper, Hudson Institute, March 12, 2010, http://www.hudson.org/files/publications/Organizing_the_USG_to_Counter_Hostile_Ideologies.pdf.

[174] Mumtaz Ahmad, "Some Random Thoughts on Religious Freedom in Pakistan," Hampton University, May 10, 2010.

[175] Chris Seiple, "Memo to the State," p. 41.

[176] Peter Harrison, *"Religion" and the Religions in the English Enlightenment* (Cambridge: Cambridge University Press, 1990), p.1.

[177] For example, at the end of the 19th century, Europeans tried to emphasize their Aryan heritage by "hellenizing" Christianity and emphasizing the universal nature of the religion. They found it simultaneously necessary to "Semitize" Islam and to associate it with the Arabs, despite knowing that most Muslims were not Arab. As Masuzawa explains, "Notwithstanding the long-established internationality and multiculturality of this religion, then, Islam came to stand as the epitome of the racially and ethnically determined, nonuniversal religions." Tomoko Masuzawa, *The Invention of World Religions: Or, How European Universalism Was Preserved in the Language of Pluralism* (Chicago: The University of Chicago Press, 2005), p. xiii, 19, 20.

[178] Russell T. McCutcheon, *Critics Not Caretakers: Redescribing the Public Study of Religion* (Albany: State University of New York Press: 2001), p. 10.

[179] Ibid., p. 61.

[180] Wilfred Cantwell Smith, "Philosophia, as One of the Religious Traditions of Humankind: The Greek Legacy in Western Civilization, Viewed by a Comparativist," in Jean-Claude Galey, ed., *Differences, valeurs, hierarchie: texts offerts a Louis Dumont* (Paris: Editions de l'Ecole des Hautes Etudes en Sciences Sociales, 1984) p. 257, as cited in Benson Saler, *Conceptualizing Religion: Immanent Anthropologists, Transcendent Natives, and Unbounded Categories* (New York: Berghahn Books, 1993), p. 215.

[181] Winnifred F. Sullivan in "Religious Persecution as a U.S. Policy Issue," p. 48.

[182] Talal Asad, *Genealogies of Religion: Discipline and Reasons of Power in Christianity and Islam* (Baltimore: The Johns Hopkins University Press, 1993), p. 28, 205.

[183] Asad, *Genealogies*, p. 234.

[184] Khaled Abou El Fadl, "The Human Rights Commitment in Modern Islam" in Joseph Runzo, Nancy M. Martin, and Arvind Sharma, eds., *Human Rights and Responsibilities in the World Religions* (Oxford: Oneworld Publications, 2002).

[185] Saba Mahmood, "The Politics of Freedom: Geopolitics, Minority Rights, and Gender," speech, Barnard College, November 5, 2009.

[186] Officials at U.S. Embassy Egypt, interview with the author, Cairo, August 2010.

[187] *Universal Declaration of Human Rights*, Article 18.

[188] See the Oslo Coalition on Freedom of Religion or Belief, http://www.oslocoalition.org/.

[189] Farr (Director of Religious Freedom Project, Berkley Center for Religion, Peace, and World Affairs), interview with the author, Washington, D.C., October 2009.

[190] Cornelis (Kees) Hulsman, (Former Director, Center for Intercultural Dialogue and Translation and Editor-in-Chief, Arab-West Report), interview with the author, Cairo, August 2010.

[191] Farr points out that tolerance can imply putting up with something undesirable, and that "in early modern Europe, the language of tolerance was used by confessional states…to describe a legal concession to certain Christian minorities." Farr, *World of Faith and Freedom*, p. 10, 128.

[192] Ibid., p. 13. Also, as Emile Nakhleh notes, "Saudi Arabia will not play if they hear we are pushing for the rights of the Shia minority—neither will Egypt, with its Coptic minority; Malaysia, with its Darul Arqam minority; nor Turkey, with its Alawite minority." Nakhleh, "Engagement for the Common Good."

[193] Jodi Breisler (Assistant Information Officer, U.S. Embassy, Greece) and Alanna Rosenberg (Political Officer, U.S. Embassy, Greece), interview with the author, Athens, August 2010.

[194] Farr and Hoover, "The Future of U.S. International Religious Freedom Policy," p. 35.

[195] Abdulaziz Sachedina, *The Islamic Roots of Democratic Pluralism* (New York: Oxford University Press, 2001), p. 13-14.

[196] Peter Nasuti, Philip J. Reiner, and Joshua T. White, "A Strategy for Hearts and Minds in South and Central Asia," *Review of Faith and International Affairs*, Fall 2008, p. 60. In Judaism as well, "human dignity" or "justice" might be more resonant than "rights," a word that has no equivalent in classical Hebrew.

[197] Maneeza Hossain, *Broken Pendulum: Bangladesh's Swing to Radicalism* (Washington, D.C.: Hudson Institute, 2007), p. 26.

[198] Rosaline Costa (Human Rights Advocate and Coordinator, Hotline Human Rights Bangladesh), interview with the author, Dhaka, April 2010.

[199] Ibid.

[200] Jared Daugherty and Hien Vu, "Engaging Communist East Asia: Recommendations for Religious Freedom," *Review of Faith and International Affairs*, Fall 2008, p. 70.

[201] Hamrin, "A New Framework for Promoting Religious Freedom in China."

[202] Muhammad Gohar (Chairman, Video Cairo SAT), interview with the author, Cairo, August 2010; Hesham Kanona, (Regional English Language Office, Office of Cultural Affairs, U.S. Embassy, Egypt), interview with the author, Cairo, August 2010.

[203] Muhammad Yousri, (Civic Unit Media Manager, Video Cairo SAT), interview with the author, Cairo, August 2010.

[204] Rokhsana Khondker, (Executive Director, Khan Foundation), interview with the author, Dhaka, April 2010.

[205] "Engaging Religious Communities Abroad," p. 45-46.

[206] Jeff Sharlet, "Jesus Killed Mohammed: The Crusade for a Christian Military," *Harper's Magazine*, May 2009, http://www.harpers.org/archive/2009/05/0082488.

[207] Farr, *World of Faith and Freedom*, p. 39.

[208] Ibid., p. 122, 127.

[209] In USCIRF's annual reports from 2001 and 2002, almost all "totalitarian" countries cited for religious persecution include specific mention of Christians or Christian denominations. U.S. Commission on International Religious Freedom, *2001 Annual Report*, May 2001, http://www.uscirf.gov/images/stories/pdf/Annual_Report/2001annRpt.pdf; U.S. Commission on International Religious Freedom, *2002 Annual Report*, May 2002, http://www.uscirf.gov/images/stories/pdf/Annual_Report/2002report.pdf.

[210] Gunn in "Religious Persecution as a U.S. Policy Issue," p. 48-50.

[211] Farr has pointedly asked, "Would anyone make the case that the postwar human rights regime is illegitimate because it originated in outrage against the treatment of Jews?" Farr, Thomas F., "Religious Freedom: Where lies wisdom, where folly?" The Immanent Frame, February 14, 2011, http://blogs.ssrc.org/tif/2011/02/14/where-lies-wisdom-where-folly/.

[212] Ibid.

[213] See Recommended Resources, p. 68.

[214] Farr, *World of Faith and Freedom*, p. 131.

[215] Albertson, "After Cairo," p. 8.

[216] Sullivan in "Religious Persecution as a U.S. Policy Issue," p. 47.

[217] Ibid.

[218] U.S. Department of State, Bureau of Democracy, Human Rights, and Labor, International Religious Freedom Office, *International Religious Freedom Report 2009*, October 26, 2009, http://www.state.gov/g/drl/rls/irf/2009/index.htm.

[219] Imam Feisal Abdul Rauf, remarks at "Religion in American Politics and Society: A Model for Other Countries?" Berkley Center for Religion, Peace, and World Affairs, Georgetown University, February 23, 2011.

[220] Grim and Finke, *Price of Freedom Denied*, p. 59.

[221] The rise may have resulted from increased anti-Muslim sentiment after September 11 and prohibitive legislation and policies under the USA PATRIOT Act, as well as increased monitoring mechanisms and

public awareness about civil liberties. "The Status of Muslim Civil Rights in the United States 2005: Unequal Protection," Council on American-Islamic Relations, 2005, p. 5, 6, http://www.cair.com/CivilRights/CivilRightsReports/2005Report.aspx.

[222] See "Civil Rights Reports," Council on American-Islamic Relations, http://www.cair.com/CivilRights/CivilRightsReports.aspx.

[223] "Draft Report of the Working Group on the Universal Periodic Review: United States of America," United Nations General Assembly, November 10, 2010, p. 17, 19, 20, 28, http://www.aclu.org/files/assets/2010-11-10-USUPRHRCREPORTRecommendations.pdf.

[224] *National Security Strategy of the United States*, p. 36.

[225] Seiple, "Ready...or Not?" p. 1.

[226] Minersville School District v. Gobitis, 310 (U.S. 586) 1940; West Virginia State Board of Education v. Barnette, 319 (U.S. 624) 1943.

[227] Grim and Finke, *Price of Freedom Denied*, p. 59.

[228] Obama, "On a New Beginning."

[229] Gunn in "Religious Persecution as a U.S. Policy Issue," p. 50.

[230] Roger Finke and Rodney Stark, *The Churching of America, 1776–2005: Winners and Losers in Our Religious Economy* (New Brunswick, NJ: Rutgers University Press, 2005).

[231] The U.S. State Department, "Report of the United States of America Submitted to the U.N. High Commissioner for Human Rights in Conjunction with the Universal Periodic Review," 2010, http://www.state.gov/documents/organization/146379.pdf.

[232] A Mission Activity Tracker (MAT) search and the Religion and Global Affairs working group report on embassy engagement with religious communities can both offer many more examples of country-specific activities, including speakers, interfaith dinners and visits by government officials to religious groups or events.

[233] Lee Rowland suggests that effective influence campaigns must be based on data-driven audience analysis and cultural insights derived from adopting an audience-centric perspective. Lee Rowland, "Effective Influence and Strategic Communication: Some Conjectured First Principles," MountainRunner, October 25, 2010, http://mountainrunner.us/2010/10/effective-influence-and-strategic-communication.html?utm_source=feedburner&utm_medium=email&utm_campaign=Feed%3A+Mountain runner+%28MountainRunner%29.

[234] Joey R. Hood (First Secretary for Press, Education, and Cultural Affairs at the U.S. Embassy in Qatar), interview with the author, June 2010.

[235] A comprehensive guide to relevant multilateral organizations can be found in Thames, Seiple and Rowe, *International Religious Freedom Advocacy.*

[236] Richard W. Timm (Catholic Educator, Hotline Human Rights Bangladesh), interview with the author, Dhaka, April 2010.

[237] Raiqah Walie-Khan (Head of Performance, Marketing & Communications, British Council, Bangladesh), interview with the author, Dhaka, April 2010.

[238] For example, in the Chinese case, "a positive Chinese response to any outside effort is easier to mobilize and justify internally if it is not primarily an American initiative pushing uniquely American values. A regional or international effort instead provides an opportunity for China to engage in internationally accepted behavior on a voluntary basis rather than under duress." Hamrin, "A New Framework for Promoting Religious Freedom in China," p. 9.

[239] Among the organizations working on interfaith efforts are: North American Interfaith Network, Council for a Parliament of the World's Religions, Tripartite Forum on Interfaith Cooperation for Peace, Committee of Religious Non-Governmental Organizations at the United Nations, World Religions Summit, The Institute of Interfaith Dialogue, the Tanenbaum Center for Interreligious Understanding, and the World Congress of Religions for Peace. See "Berkley Center Knowledge Resources," Berkley Center for Religion, Peace, and World Affairs, http://berkleycenter.georgetown.edu/resources, and "Resources," The Pluralism Project at Harvard University, http://pluralism.org/resources/index.php.

[240] Discussion at "Minutes of the U.S. Advisory Commission on Public Diplomacy July 2010 Official Meeting," U.S. Department of State, July 20, 2010, http://www.state.gov/r/adcompd/146252.htm.

[241] Those goals would fit into the third category of a model for public diplomacy evaluation based on three goals: increasing understanding of the United States, increasing favorability toward the United States and increasing U.S. influence in the world. Kenneth Matwiczak, "Public Diplomacy: Model for the Assessment

of Performance," Report to the U.S. Advisory Commission on Public Diplomacy, Lyndon B. Johnson School of Public Affairs, University of Texas at Austin, September 2010.

[242] Heshaam Kanona (Regional English Language Office, Office of Cultural Affairs, U.S. Embassy, Egypt), interview with the author, Cairo, August 2010.

[243] Dr. Abdeldayem Nossair (Special Advisor to the Grand Imam, General Secretary of World Association of Al-Azhar Graduates, Al-Azhar University's Advisor for Development of IT and Languages), interview with the author, Cairo, August 2010.

[244] Kanona, interview.

[245] Jeanette Coogan (Manager, Al Azhar English Training Centre, British Council, Egypt), Cairo, August 2010.

[246] Ali Gomaa, "Islam, Israel, and the United States," *Wall Street Journal*, October 7, 2009, http://online.wsj.com/article/SB10001424052748703298004574457452301729982.html.

[247] Shereef Mohammed Edreis, Abdel-Rahman Hassan, Khaled M. Hemaya, Mostafa Abdul Karim, Ahmed Adly Said, Shereef Tawfik (Cairo-based imams), interview with the author, Cairo, August 2010.

[248] Syed Nazrul Ahsan, Javed Hyder Kareem, Khan Md. Sabbir (Language Proficiency Center), interview with the author, Dhaka, April 2010.

[249] With a GDP per capita under $1,700 in 2010, Bangladesh is one of the poorest countries in the world. It is also a very young nation: the median age there is 22.9 years. "Bangladesh," CIA World Factbook, February 11, 2011, https://www.cia.gov/library/publications/the-world-factbook/geos/bg.html.

[250] For more information about the Asia Foundation's Leaders of Influence program, see "Leaders of Influence," The Asia Foundation, http://asiafoundation.org/media/view/video/0ERrN7Ddci8/leaders-of-influence.

[251] See "Building Collaborative Communities: Enhancing Cooperation Among People of Different Faiths," Religions for Peace, January 2010, http://religionsforpeace.org/news/press/building-collaborative.html.

[252] "Religion, Conflict & Peacebuilding," USAID, p. 27.

[253] Ibid., p. 28.

[254] See http://clergybeyondborders.org/ for more information.

[255] As Hannah Rosenthal, U.S. special envoy to monitor and combat anti-Semitism, said before Congress, "Holocaust denial doesn't just feed anti-Semitism; Holocaust denial is a form of anti-Semitism." Hannah Rosenthal, speech, "Confronting Religious Bigotry, Anti-Semitism, and Holocaust Denial," Washington, D.C., September 22, 2010, http://www.state.gov/g/drl/rls/rm/2010/147891.htm.

[256] Hannah Rosenthal (Special Envoy, Office to Monitor and Combat Anti-Semitism), interview with the author, Washington, D.C., July 2010.

[257] Rosenthal, "Confronting Religious Bigotry, Anti-Semitism, and Holocaust Denial."

[258] Another participant, Marshall Breger, a former special assistant to President Reagan, told a reporter that "it is important to reach out to Muslims prepared to talk to us, people who are ready to open themselves to experiences which might be transformative for them—as occurred on this trip to Dachau and Auschwitz." Laura Rozen, "Imams Join U.S. Officials at Nazi Sites," *Politico*, August 18, 2010, http://www.politico.com/news/stories/0810/41220.html.

[259] Examples of religious leaders who have been very active in religious reconciliation and other peacemaking can be found in David Little, ed., *Peacemakers in Action: Profiles of Religion in Conflict Resolution* (Cambridge: Cambridge University Press, 2007).

[260] A major "product" that the United States can export is strategy for the development of civil society through partnerships and coalitions. Rosenthal, interview.

[261] The U.S. government has been involved in similar projects abroad. A USAID-sponsored, privately run reality television program called *Dream and Achieve* airs weekly on Tolo TV, Afghanistan's most popular station. On the show, Afghan entrepreneurs compete for financial support for their businesses, inspiring further entrepreneurship and innovation in Afghanistan. Megan Goldin, "Reality TV Show Stirs Business Spirit In Afghanistan," Tolo TV, September 2, 2008, http://tolo.tv/content/view/247/42/lang,english/.

[262] See http://www.sfcg.org/programmes/cgp/programmes_cgp.html

[263] Nigeria's population of 138 million is believed to be almost evenly divided between Muslims and Christians. Internal migration has resulted in Christians and Muslims' living alongside one another in an increasing number of "fault line" cities. Fighting over land ownership and political representation has led to the deaths of tens of thousands of people since 1999, and "Christian" and "Islamic" militias have sprung up to defend sectarian interests.

[264] Gohar, interview. Leon Shahabian (Vice President and Treasurer, Layalina Productions), interview with the author, Washington, DC, October 2009.

[265] *"On the Road in America* Season 1," Layalina Productions, http://www.layalina.tv/productions/ontheroad.html.

[266] See http://www.videocairosat.com/cms.php?id=landing_page

[267] See Abdurrahman Wahid, "Islam, Pluralism and Democracy," tr. Mark Woodward, Consortium for Strategic Communication, Arizona State University, April 19, 2007, http://comops.org/article/113.pdf.

[268] See http://www.citylore.org/events/illuminated_2011/verses.htm for more information.

[269] See http://www.oursharedeurope.org/ for more information.

[270] For more on the Sabido Methodology, see: "Sabido Methodology – Background," Population Media Center, http://www.populationmedia.org/what/sabido-method/.

[271] In 2011, for example, the National Endowment for the Humanities has invited proposals through its *Bridging Cultures* initiative for projects that use documentary films to examine international and transnational themes, including international religious issues.

[272] Michael Hankey (Assistant Cultural Affairs Officer, U.S. Embassy, Egypt), interview with the author, Cairo, August 2010.

[273] Jennifer Bryson (Director of the Islam and Civil Society Project, Witherspoon Institute), interview with the author, Washington, DC, April 2010. See also: Bryson, "Don't Forget Religious Freedom," *Public Discourse: Ethics, Law, and the Common Good*, The Witherspoon Institute, November 17, 2009, http://www.thepublicdiscourse.com/2009/11/1017.

[274] See http://www.americaabroadmedia.org/programs/view/id/133

[275] For more about MOST, see http://www.mostresource.org/

[276] "Religion, Conflict & Peacebuilding," USAID, p. 21.

[277] See http://www.cawu.org/

[278] U.S.-supported workshops for journalists in Greece, for example, have focused on covering immigration, integration and gender equality. Breisler and Rosenberg, interview.

[279] Ahmed Subhy Mansour, *Suggestions to Revise Muslim Religion Courses in Egyptian Education to Make Egyptians More Tolerant* (Cairo: Ibn Khaldoun Center, 1999).

[280] Ehsan Mahsood, "Our Shared Europe: Swapping Treasures, Sharing Losses, Celebrating Futures," British Council, 2008, p. 13, http://www.oursharedeurope.org/documents/OSE_report.pdf.

[281] Grim, interview.

[282] Jesse Lichtenstein, "Digital Diplomacy," *The New York Times Magazine*, July 2010, p. 25-29.

[283] Lowell H. Schwartz et al., "Barriers to the Broad Dissemination of Creative Works in the Arab World," RAND National Defense Research Institute, The RAND Corporation, 2009, http://www.rand.org/pubs/monographs/2009/RAND_MG879.pdf.

[284] See the IRF report's recognition of significant steps, including youth reconciliation camps and popular media, that government and non-government actors have taken toward improving religious freedom conditions. *International Religious Freedom Report 2009*.

[285] See http://institute.jesdialogue.org/programs/study_of_the_us_instituteson_religious_pluralis%20m/ for more information.

[286] "Islam and Religious Freedom: July 5-9, 2011," The Witherspoon Institute, http://www.winst.org/ethics_and_university/seminars/islam/index.php.

[287] See http://exchanges.state.gov/academicexchanges/rel_pluralism.html%20and%20http:/www.ia.ucsb.edu/pa/display.aspx?pkey=2275 for more information.

[288] See http://oneworld2011.org/

[289] Potential partners on Islam, for example, include: Islamic Society of North America, Council on American-Islamic Relations, American Islamic Congress, Free Muslim Coalition, Center for the Study of Islam & Democracy, Muslim Public Affairs Council, the University of California at Berkeley and Zeytuna College.

[290] The U.S. Center for Citizen Diplomacy (USCCD) is working toward a 10-year Initiative for Global Citizen Diplomacy that aims to double the number of American volunteers of all ages involved in international activities at home or abroad, from an estimated 60 million today to 120 million by 2020. See http://uscenterforcitizendiplomacy.org/.

[291] A popular Australian High Commission program annually brings 40 youth ambassadors, ages 20 to 35, to work in various NGOs throughout Bangladesh. Kilmeny Beckering Vinckers (Deputy High Commissioner, Australian High Commission, Bangladesh), interview with the author, May 2010.

[292] In Bangladesh, for example, U.S. chaplains are helping that country's military develop its own chaplaincy. Harvey Sernovitz (Press & Information Officer, The American Center, U.S. Embassy, Bangladesh), interview with the author, Dhaka, April 2010.

[293] Albertson, "After Cairo."

[294] Participating institutes are in Afghanistan, Bahrain, Denmark, Egypt, Finland, France, Germany, Indonesia, Italy, Jordan, Kuwait, Lebanon, Morocco, Netherlands, Norway, the Palestinian Territories, Qatar, Saudi Arabia, Tunisia, Turkey, United Arab Emirates, United Kingdom, United States and Yemen. See "Connect Program," Soliya, http://www.soliya.net/?q=connect_program.

[295] Each semester, Soliya evaluates the program based on a test designed by Intermedia, an independent firm. See "Results," Soliya, http://www.soliya.net/?q=results.

[296] See http://www.britishcouncil.org/learning-connecting-classrooms.htm for more information.

[297] See http://www.tonyblairfaithfoundation.org/pages/content-/

[298] Georgia Gould, Tony Blair Faith Foundation, email to author, July 22, 2010.

[299] Rosenthal, interview.

[300] See http://thisibelieve.org/

[301] The respective websites are: http://www.beyondtolerance.org/; http://www.patheos.com/; http://www.odysseynetworks.org/; and http://www.altmuslim.com/
For more about these sites, see "Bridging Babel: New Social Media and Interreligious and Intercultural Understanding," Berkley Center for Religion, Peace, and World Affairs, May 2010, http://berkleycenter.georgetown.edu/publications/bridging-babel-new-social-media-and-interreligious-and-intercultural-understanding.

[302] See http://www.state.gov/s/2011hoursagainsthate/

[303] Ideas from "Bridging Babel," p. 20, 34, 35.

[304] Keith Allison, remarks, "U.S. Relations with the Muslim World: One Year After Cairo," Center for the Study of Islam and Democracy 11th Annual Conference, April 28, 2010, Washington, D.C..

[305] See http://www.bylc.org/ for more information.

[306] Rebecca Knight, "Building Bridges," *Financial Times*, September 26, 2010, http://www.ft.com/cms/s/2/b6818dca-c7fd-11df-ae3a-00144feab49a,dwp_uuid=2f7ecb9c-092b-11dc-a349-000b5df10621,print=yes.html.

[307] Interfaith dialogue is a growing movement on U.S. campuses. Georgetown's Berkley Center offers an "Interfaith Dialogue on Campus" resource that tracks efforts nationally. "Interfaith Dialogue on Campus," Berkley Center for Religion, Peace, and World Affairs, http://berkleycenter.georgetown.edu/resources/topics/interreligious-dialogue/subtopics/interfaith-dialogue-on-campus.

[308] "White House Hosts IFYC Interfaith Leadership Institute," Council for a Parliament of the World's Religions, http://www.parliamentofreligions.org/news/index.php/2010/09/white-house-hosts-ifyc-interfaith-leadership-institute/.

[309] Joe Carlsmith, "Standing up for religion," *Yale Daily News*, November 13, 2009, http://www.yaledailynews.com/news/2009/nov/13/carlsmith-standing-up-for-religion/

[310] "Leadership in the Face of Religious Bigotry: A Resource for Campus Leaders," Interfaith Youth Core, pp. 5, 19.

[311] See http://www.tonyblairfaithfoundation.org/pages/1139/

[312] See http://www.britishcouncil.org/usa-science-projects-climate-champions.htm

[313] For a model program, see The OpEd Project, http://theopedproject.org/index.php?option=com_content&view=article&id=418

[314] U.S. Commission on International Religious Freedom, *2004 Annual Report*, May 2004, p. 41, http://www.uscirf.gov/images/stories/PDFs/annualreport2004may.pdf.

[315] See program description in *International Religious Freedom Advocacy, p. 139-146.*

[316] *International Religious Freedom Advocacy*, p. 142.

[317] In 2010, Seiple was invited to speak to Vietnamese Embassy staff about religious freedom and national security in the United States. He offered a three-minute case for principled pluralism and a nine-minute discussion of ethno-religious insurgencies and the role of religious leaders in deterring terrorism.

[318] ICRD was established to carry out Douglas Johnston's vision of faith-based diplomacy, articulated in his book *Faith-based Diplomacy: Trumping Realpolitik*, the sequel to the seminal *Religion, the Missing Dimension of Statecraft*, both of which make the case for religious considerations in foreign policy.

[319] Douglas M. Johnston, "Madrassa Reform Key," *Washington Times*, August 7, 2009, http://www.washingtontimes.com/news/2009/aug/7/madrassa-reform-key/.

[320] "Third-party Program Evaluation by the Salam Institute for Peace and Justice," International Center for Religion and Diplomacy, December 4, 2008, p. 3, 5, http://www.icrd.org/storage/icrd/documents/salam_institute_evaluation_final.pdf.

[321] Ibid., p. 4.

[322] Ibid., p. 5.

[323] ICRD now receives more requests for trainings than it can accommodate, but it has still been able to employ its faith-based diplomacy approach in many other places. Another notable example is their work in helping to establish the Sudan Inter-religious Council, a forum for Muslim and Christian clergy to solve problems between communities and ensure religious freedom.

[324] "Religion, Conflict & Peacebuilding," USAID, p. 16, 17.

[325] Scott Sayare, "Feeling Slighted by France, and Respected by U.S.," *New York Times*, September 22, 2010, http://www.nytimes.com/2010/09/23/world/europe/23france.html?_r=1.

[326] See USCIRF's recommendations for Southern Sudan, *2009 Annual Report*, p. 106.

[327] David Hunsicker (Conflict and Natural Resources Specialist, USAID), interview with the author, Washington, DC, December 2009.